S. Hrg. 113–699

AUTHORIZATION FOR THE USE OF MILITARY FORCE AGAINST ISIL

HEARING

BEFORE THE

COMMITTEE ON FOREIGN RELATIONS UNITED STATES SENATE

ONE HUNDRED THIRTEENTH CONGRESS

SECOND SESSION

DECEMBER 9, 2014

Printed for the use of the Committee on Foreign Relations

Available via the World Wide Web: http://www.gpo.gov/fdsys/

U.S. GOVERNMENT PUBLISHING OFFICE

95–891 PDF WASHINGTON : 2015

For sale by the Superintendent of Documents, U.S. Government Publishing Office
Internet: bookstore.gpo.gov   Phone: toll free (866) 512–1800; DC area (202) 512–1800
Fax: (202) 512–2104   Mail: Stop IDCC, Washington, DC 20402–0001

(II)

CONTENTS

(III)

AUTHORIZATION FOR THE USE OF MILITARY FORCE AGAINST ISIL

TUESDAY, DECEMBER 9, 2014

U.S. SENATE,
COMMITTEE ON FOREIGN RELATIONS,
Washington, DC.

The committee met, pursuant to notice, at 2:08 p.m., in room 106, Dirksen Senate Office Building, Hon. Robert Menendez (chairman of the committee) presiding.

Present: Senators Menendez, Boxer, Cardin, Shaheen, Coons, Durbin, Udall, Murphy, Kaine, Markey, Corker, Risch, Rubio, Johnson, Flake, McCain, Barrasso, and Paul.

OPENING STATEMENT OF HON. ROBERT MENENDEZ, U.S. SENATOR FROM NEW JERSEY

The CHAIRMAN. This committee will come to order. Mr. Secretary, we welcome you back to the committee, and we thank you for being here today to discuss one of the most important challenges that Congress must meet.

When you last appeared before this committee in September, you asked Congress to authorize the use of military force against ISIL, and we have an AUMF that the committee will consider later this week. Today we are asking you to provide the administration's views on this text and on your strategic planning to counter ISIL along with the range of military authorities you will need to achieve your goals.

This is the most important vote that any member of Congress can take. It is a vote that potentially sends America's sons and daughters into harm's way, and we do not take that responsibility lightly. That reality demands our full attention and consideration of three issues. First, whether military action to counter ISIL is necessary and in the national security interests of the United States. I believe that it is, and I doubt anyone on the committee would disagree. I believe that the risk of ISIL acquiring a safe haven in Iraq or Syria or beyond from which it can create the operational capacity to attack American interests and, at some point, America itself demands action. Second, we need to understand the political and military goals of this operation, how we expect to achieve them, and the timeframe of this campaign.

Now, I know some may see this as limiting, but at the end of the day Americans will not be supportive of an authorization of an endless war. They do not want us to occupy Iraq for decades. They do not want an ISIL recruitment AUMF allowing ISIL to claim a jihad against Western crusaders that enhances their ability to recruit followers who want to fight Americans. In my view, deployment of ground troops at this time would be Groundhog Day in Iraq all over again. Lastly, we need to hear what authorities the Commander in Chief expects that he will need from Congress to achieve his political and military goals of defeating ISIL and closing the region to extremists and terrorists.

Now, frankly, the process we undertake today is not the one I sought. I had hoped to begin this conversation weeks ago so that the entire Senate, not just this committee, would have time to consider a comprehensive bipartisan AUMF. But that did not happen, and we are here today to begin the process of taking action. I think the American people expect their congressional leaders to engage fully on this issue, to understand the mission, the parameters, and the risks.

As I have said many times, I am not comfortable with the administration's reliance on the 9/11 AUMF and the 2002 Iraq AUMF. The 9/11 AUMF was adopted to counter al-Qaeda in the wake of the September 11 attacks. No member could have foreseen that we would still be acting under its authority 13 years later. I do not believe that it provides the authority to pursue a new enemy in different countries under completely different circumstances than existed 13 years ago.

Congress, rather than the Executive, has the responsibility and the authority to authorize military action and to declare war for these very reasons. We are the check and balance on Executive power regardless of who that Executive is, and if we abandon that role, then we will have done a grave disservice to the American people.

The text that I have presented is based on consultations with members of the committee and addresses the authorities we understand the White House is seeking. In my view, an ISIL-specific AUMF should in broad terms authorize the President to use military force against ISIL and associated persons or forces, meaning individuals or organizations, fighting for, or on behalf of, ISIL. It should limit the activities of our forces so that there will be no large-scale ground combat operations. If the President feels he needs that, then he should ask for it and Congress can consider it. It should limit the authorization to 3 years, and it should require the administration to report to Congress every 60 days.

As drafted, the text would limit the authorization of force by not allowing ground combat operations except as necessary for the protection or rescue of U.S. soldiers or citizens, for intelligence operations, spotters to enable airstrikes, operational planning, or other forms of advice and assistance. The authorization would be limited to 3 years.

The President has said that this will be a multiyear campaign, but I do not believe that the AUMF should be unlimited. A 3-year timeframe would allow this President and a new President time to assess the situation and make a responsible decision together with the Congress about whether and how to continue military action. So that said, Mr. Secretary, we would love to hear from the administration what the framework is, what you see as the U.S.-led strategy to counter ISIL.

Finally, let me conclude by saying I do not believe that placing limitations in this AUMF sends a message of weakness to our enemies. This authorization is intended to provide the authority required by the Commander in Chief to do our part in this multinational effort to defeat ISIL. ISIL is not only an American problem. It is a global problem, and no ISIL strategy can rely on American military power alone. We need to train Iraqi Security Forces and Kurdish Peshmerga forces; stand up and train and equip programs for moderate Syrian fighters, which are being authorized in the defense authorization bill that the Congress will consider this week, work with coalition partners to cut off terror financing and foreign fighter flows, and provide humanitarian aid to address the urgent, desperate situation of millions in the region whose lives have been uprooted.

We look forward to working with you, Mr. Secretary, and the administration on our mutual goal of degrading and defeating ISIL. And, again, we welcome you back to the committee. Let me turn to the distinguished ranking member for his remarks, Senator Corker.

OPENING STATEMENT OF HON. BOB CORKER, U.S. SENATOR FROM TENNESSEE

Senator CORKER. Mr. Chairman, thank you for allowing us to move away from what we considered last week, which was an AUMF that was an amendment to a water bill. I think that is a step forward, and I appreciate you doing that. I want to thank the Secretary for being here. I am not sure that—matter of fact, I am pretty sure this is not where he would like to be this afternoon, so I thank you for coming before our committee.

And I want to thank the chairman again for trying to set up a process this week that was thorough, but that has not occurred, and I think everyone understands that some of the things that will be discussed obviously are things like boots on the ground, and yet we have no defense presentations here. We have no intelligence presentations here.

And I would also say that back in the Syrian issue, the original Syrian issue, about a year and a half ago, where we were authorizing something that—these are my words—was going to last about 10 hours, we were able to go through a process that was much more serious than the one we are going to have this week. I think all of us know that whatever passes out of the committee this week is not going to become law. I agree with some comments that the chairman and I had earlier, and that is, well, at least this will be a part of a process, and I thank him for saying that, and I agree with that.

At the same time, just for what it is worth, I do not think—I know we are not going to get to a place where the House and Senate pass an authorization. And I just want to say we weaken our Nation when we begin a process like that and we do not actually enact it in law. We weaken our Nation. I think we also hurt our Nation when we attempt to pass something out on a partisan basis. One of the things about the earlier Syrian AUMF was it had bipartisan support and bipartisan opposition. So, for what it is worth, regardless of what happens in these meetings this week, my plan of conduct personally is to act in such a way that hopefully will not harden positions, but will build for an opportunity for us to act in a more full way down the road.

I do want to say that I think the testimony today will be helpful. I listened to the chairman's comments and then refer to the fact that the 60-word authorization that was passed September the 18th of 2001 has led to some outcomes that people did not anticipate. And that is why from my standpoint I would like to have something much more full, much more understood, a strategy that is laid out in a way that I understand where we are going prior to authorizing a complete authorization. If you look at our Nation since World War II, we have had multiple conflicts. It is hard to remember one that ended up with a very satisfactory outcome. What we do is we tend to start these conflicts without really teasing out from the administration in most cases how we are going to actually go about being successful, so we start the process.

In this particular case, it appears that an AUMF has been offered to start the process that actually limits the Commander in Chief's ability to carry it out. As a matter of fact, what would happen under this authorization is right now we can use all efforts, if you will, to go against al-Qaeda, but if we were to pass this authorization as written, we would be saying against ISIS we can only do certain things, that somehow we must view them as being a lesser evil than the al-Qaeda effort—the al-Qaeda group that we have gone after and the Taliban group that we have gone after in Afghanistan.

I hope that, again, we will all conduct ourselves in a manner this week that will not harden positions. We are not going to do anything that passes, unfortunately. I do not think that is good for our Nation. I think it is better to start this at a time we can finish it with a Congress, by the way, that will actually deal with this from start to finish. But I do appreciate, again, the chairman deferring to this week trying to make the process slightly better. And I certainly appreciate, in spite of the fact we do not have a full presentation, I appreciate Secretary Kerry being here today and making the presentation he is going to make.

The CHAIRMAN. Mr. Secretary.

STATEMENT OF HON. JOHN F. KERRY, SECRETARY, U.S. DEPARTMENT OF STATE, WASHINGTON, DC

Secretary KERRY. Well, Mr. Chairman, and Ranking Member Corker, and all my former colleagues, it is really is a pleasure for me to be back before the Foreign Relations Committee.

You know, during my time here, I think we got some things right. We certainly wound up wishing we had done some things differently. But I think most of us would agree, and I saw it during both parties' chairmanships, including the years that Senator Lugar and I were here, that this committee works best and makes the greatest contribution to our foreign policy and our country when it addresses the most important issues in a strong, bipartisan fashion, and this is one of those issues. The chairman and the ranking member have both said that. This is one of the moments when a bipartisan approach really is critical.

As you know, the President is committed to engaging with the committee and all of your colleagues in the House and Senate regarding a new authorization for the use of military force—as we call it in short, the AUMF—specifically against the terrorist group known as ISIL, though in the region it is called Daesh, and specifically because they believe very deeply it is not a state, and it does not represent Islam.

So we are looking for this authorization with respect to efforts against Daesh and affiliated groups. And I want to thank Chairman Menendez and the entire committee for leading the effort in Congress and for all of the important work that you have already done on this complicated and challenging issue. It is important that this committee lead the Congress and the country, and I think you know I believe that.

Now, I realize we may not get there overnight. I have heard the ranking member's comments just now, and we understand the clock. We certainly will not resolve everything and get there this afternoon in the next few hours. But I do think this discussion is important, and I think we all agree that this discussion has to conclude with a bipartisan vote that makes clear that this is not one party's fight against Daesh, but rather that it reflects our united determination to degrade and ultimately defeat Daesh.

And the world needs to understand that from the U.S. Congress above all.

Our coalition partners need to know that from all of you, and the men and women of our armed forces deserve to know it from all of you, and Daesh's cadre of killers and rapist and bigots need to absolutely understand it clearly. That is why this matters. Now, toward that end, we ask you now to work closely with us on a bipartisan basis to develop language that provides a clear signal of support for our ongoing military operations against Daesh.

Our position on the text is really pretty straightforward. The authorization, or AUMF, should give the President the clear mandate and the flexibility he needs to successfully prosecute the armed conflict against Daesh and affiliated forces, but the authorization should also be limited and specific to the threat posed by that group and by forces associated with it. Now, I will come back to the question of the AUMF in a minute. But we believe that as we embark on this important discussion, context matters. All of us want to see the United States succeed, and all of us want to see Daesh defeated, so we are united on that. And I want to bring the committee up to date on precisely where our campaign now stands.

Mr. Chairman, less than 3 months ago, perhaps 2½ months, perhaps a little more, have passed since the international community came together in a coalition whose purpose is to degrade and defeat Daesh. Two and a half months ago it did not exist—not ''it'' Daesh, but the coalition and the 60 countries that assembled recently in Brussels. We organized, and I had the privilege of chairing, the first ministerial level meeting of the coalition last week in Brussels. We heard Iraqi Prime Minister al-Abadi describe to us the effort that his leadership team is making to bring Iraqis together, strengthen their security forces, take the fight to Daesh, and improve and reform governance. We also heard Gen. John Allen, our special envoy to the coalition, review the progress that is being made in the five lines of coalition effort: to shrink the territory controlled by Daesh, to cut off its financing, to block its recruitment of foreign fighters, to expose the hypocrisy of its absurd religious claims, and to provide humanitarian aid to the victims of its violence.

During the meeting, I have to tell you I was particularly impressed by the leadership activism, and, quite frankly, the anger toward Daesh that is being displayed by Arab and Muslim states. Governments that do not always agree on other issues are coming together in opposition to this profoundly anti-Islamic terrorist organization. And now, to be clear, ISIL continues to commit serious, vicious crimes, and it still controls more territory than al-Qaeda ever did. It will be years, not months, before it is defeated. We know that. But our coalition is measurably already making a difference.

To date, we have launched more than 1,150 today airstrikes against Daesh. These operations have reduced its leadership, undermined its propaganda, squeezed its resources, damaged its logistical and operational capabilities, and compelled it to disperse its forces and change its tactics. It is becoming clear that the combination of coalition airstrikes and local ground partners is a potent one. In fact, virtually every time a local Iraqi force has worked in coordination with our air cover, they have not only defeated Daesh, they have routed it.

In Iraq, progress also continues in the political arena, and this is no less important frankly. Last week after years of intensive efforts, the Government in Baghdad reached an interim accord with the Kurdistan regional government on hydrocarbon exports and revenue-sharing. That has been long sought after, and it is a big deal that they got it. It is good for the country's economy, but it is even better for its unity and stability and for the imprint of the direction that they are moving in.

In addition, the new Defense Minister is a Sunni, whose appointment was an important step toward a more inclusive government. And with his leadership, and that of the new Interior Minister, the process of reforming the nation's security forces has a genuine chance for success. Meanwhile, the Prime Minister is taking bold steps to improve relations with his country's neighbors, and those neighbors, including Saudi Arabia, the UAE, and Turkey, have been responding. Now, I want to underscore, it is too early to declare a new era in regional relations. But countries that had been drifting apart or even in conflict with each other, are now in the process of coming together and breaking down the barriers that were created. And that is helpful to our coalition, and it is bad news for Daesh.

Beating back the threat that Daesh poses to Iraq is job number one for our Iraqi partners and for our coalition. But even if the Government in Baghdad fulfills its responsibilities, it is still going to face a dire challenge because of the events in Syria. Now, if you recall, the coalition's decision to carry out airstrikes in Syria came in response to a request from Iraq for help in defending against Daesh's brazen attack. To date, we and our Arab partners have conducted over 500 airstrikes in Syria, targeting areas where Daesh had concentrated its fighters, targeting on command and control nodes, finance centers, training camps, and oil refineries. Our objective is to further degrade Daesh's capabilities and to deny it the freedom of movement and resupply that it has previously enjoyed.

At the same time, we will continue to build up the capabilities of the moderate opposition, and here I want to thank the members of this committee and many others in Congress who have supported these efforts and supported them very strongly. Our goal is to help the moderate forces stabilize areas under their control, defend civilians, empower them to go on offense against Daesh, and promote the conditions for a negotiated political transition, recognizing, as I think almost every person has said, there no military solution.

Now, Mr. Chairman, we all know that Daesh is a threat to America's security and interests. It poses an unaccepted danger to our personnel and facilities in Iraq and elsewhere. It seeks to destroy both the short- and long-term stability of the broader Middle East, and it is exacerbating a refugee crisis that has placed extraordinary economic and political burden on our friends and allies in the region.

One thing is certain. Daesh will continue to spread until or unless it is stopped. So there should be no question that we, with our partners, have a moral duty and a profound international security interest and national security interest in stopping them. That is where the fight against Daesh now stands. A coalition that 2½ months ago did not even exist is now taking the fight to the enemy. It was cobbled together by strong American leadership and by steady, intensive diplomacy with countries that disagree on many things, but all share an aversion to extremism.

Now, I think all of you would agree, we need to summon that same determination to find the common ground here in Washington. And that is why in the hours, days, and weeks to come we are determined to work with you, first and foremost to develop an approach that can generate broad bipartisan support, while ensuring that the President has the flexibility to successfully prosecute this effort. That is the balance.

What do we envision specifically regarding an AUMF? Importantly, and I think I will lay out today a very clear set of principles that I hope will be instructive, we do not think an AUMF should include a geographic limitation. We do not anticipate conducting operations in countries other than Iraq or Syria, but to the extent that ISIL poses a threat to American interests and personnel in other countries, we would not want an AUMF to constrain our ability to use appropriate force against ISIL in those locations if necessary. In our view, it would be a mistake to advertise to ISIL that there are safe havens for them outside of Iraq or Syria.

On the issue of combat operations, I know this is hotly debated, as it ought to be and as it is, with passionate and persuasive arguments on both sides. The President has been crystal clear that his policy is that U.S. military forces will not be deployed to conduct ground combat operations against ISIL, and that will be the responsibility of local forces because that is what our local partners and allies want. That is what we learned works best in the context of our Iraq experience. That is what is best for preserving our coalition, and, most importantly, it is in the best interests of the United States. However, while we certainly believe that this is the soundest possible policy, and while the President has been clear he is open to clarifications on the use of U.S. combat troops to be outlined in an AUMF, it does not mean that we should preemptively bind the hands of the Commander in Chief or our commanders in the field in responding to scenarios and contingencies that are impossible to foresee.

And finally, with respect to duration, we can be sure that this confrontation is not going to be over quickly, as the President and I have said many times. We understand, however, the desire of many to avoid a completely open-ended authorization. And I note that Chairman Menendez has suggested that a 3-year limitation should be put into an AUMF. We support that proposal, but we support it subject to a provision that we should work through together that provides for extension in the event that circumstances require it, and we think it ought to be advertised as such up front.

To sum up, Mr. Chairman and members of the committee, I ask for your help in, above all, approving on a bipartisan basis with the strongest vote possible because everybody will read messages into that vote, an authorization for use of military force in connection with our campaign and that of our many partners in order to defeat a terrible, vicious, different kind of enemy. Almost a quarter of a century ago when I was here, then a 47-year-old Senator with certainly a darker head of hair, President George H.W. Bush, sent his Secretary of State, James Baker, to ask this committee for the authority to respond militarily to the Iraqi invasion of Kuwait. The country was divided. Congress was divided. But this committee drafted an authorization, and it passed the Congress with a majority that the New York Times described as decisive and bipartisan. And armed with that mandate, Secretary Baker built the coalition that won the first gulf war.

Now, that was a different time, and it was a different conflict, and it called for a different response. But it was also this body, this committee and then the Senate, at its bipartisan best. And what we need from you today to strengthen and unify our own coalition is exactly that kind of cooperative effort. The world will be watching what we together are willing and able to do, and this, obviously, is not a partisan issue. It is a leadership issue. It is a test of our government's ability and our Nation's ability to stand together. It is a test of our generation's resolve to build a safer and more secure world. And I know every single one of you wants to defeat ISIL.

A bold bipartisan mandate would strengthen our hand, and I hope that today you can move close to that goal. So thank you, and I am pleased to answer any questions.

[The prepared statement of Secretary Kerry follows:]

PREPARED STATEMENT OF SECRETARY OF STATE JOHN F. KERRY

Mr. Chairman, Ranking Member Corker—Senators—good afternoon, thank you for having me back to the Foreign Relations Committee.

During my time here, we got many things right, and some things we wish we had done differently. But I think that most of us would agree—and I saw it during both parties' chairmanships, including the years Senator Lugar and I were here—that this committee works best, and makes the greatest contribution to our foreign policy, when it addresses the most important issues on a strong, bipartisan basis.

This is one of those issues, and one of those moments, when that approach is critical.

As you know, the President is committed to engaging with this committee and your colleagues in the Senate and House of Representatives regarding a new Authorization to Use Military Force against the terrorist group known as ISIL and affiliated groups. I want to thank Chairman Menendez and the entire committee for leading this effort in Congress and for all of the important work you have already done on this complicated and challenging issue.

I realize we may not get there overnight—and we certainly won't resolve everything and get there this afternoon. But I think we all agree that this discussion must conclude with a bipartisan vote that makes clear that this is not one party's fight against ISIL but rather that it reflects our unified determination to degrade and ultimately defeat ISIL. Our coalition partners need to know it. The men and women of our armed forces need to know it. And ISIL's cadres of killers, rapists, and bigots need to understand it.

Toward that end, we ask you now to work closely with us on a bipartisan basis to develop language that provides a clear signal of support for our ongoing military operations against ISIL.

Our position on the text is pretty straightforward—the Authorization—or AUMF—should give the President the clear mandate and flexibility he needs to successfully prosecute the armed conflict against ISIL and affiliated forces; but the Authorization should also be limited and specific to the threat posed by that group and by forces associated with it.

I will return to the question of the AUMF in a minute, but as we embark on this important discussion, context matters. All of us want to see the United States succeed and ISIL to be defeated, and I want to bring the committee up to date on where our campaign now stands.

Mr. Chairman, less than 3 months have passed since the international community came together in a coalition whose purpose is to degrade and defeat ISIL. This past Wednesday, in Brussels, we organized and I had the privilege of chairing the first ministerial-level meeting of that coalition. We heard Iraqi Prime Minister Abadi describe to us the effort that his leadership team is making to bring Iraqis together, strengthen their security forces, take the fight to ISIL, and improve and reform governance. We also heard General John Allen, our special envoy, review the progress that is being made in the five lines of coalition effort: to shrink the territory controlled by ISIL, cut off its financing, block its recruitment of foreign fighters, expose the hypocrisy of its absurd religious claims, and provide humanitarian aid to the victims of its violence.

During the meeting, I was especially impressed by the leadership, activism and quite frankly, the anger toward ISIL that is being displayed by Arab and Muslim states. Governments that do not always agree on other issues are coming together in opposition to this profoundly anti-Islamic terrorist organization.

Now, to be clear: ISIL continues to commit vicious crimes and it still controls more territory than al-Qaeda ever did. It will be years, not months, before it is defeated. But our coalition is already making a big difference.

To date, we have launched more than 1,100 air strikes against ISIL targets. These operations have reduced ISIL's leadership, undermined its propaganda, squeezed its resources, damaged its logistical and operational capabilities, and compelled it to disperse its forces and change its tactics. It is becoming clear that the combination of coalition air strikes and local ground partners is a potent one. In fact, virtually every time a local Iraqi force has worked in coordination with our air cover, they've not only defeated ISIL; they've routed ISIL.

In Iraq, progress also continues in the political arena. Last week, after years of intensive efforts, the government in Baghdad reached an interim accord with the Kurdistan Regional Government on hydrocarbon exports and revenue-sharing. That is good for the country's economy but even more for its unity and stability. In addition, the new Defense Minister is a Sunni whose appointment was an important step toward a more inclusive government. With his leadership and that of the new Interior Minister, the process of reforming the nation's security forces has a genuine chance for success.

Meanwhile, the Prime Minister is taking bold steps to improve relations with his country's neighbors—and those neighbors including Saudi Arabia, the UAE, and Turkey—have been responding. It's too early to declare a new era in regional relations, but countries that had been drifting apart are in the process of coming together. That's helpful to our coalition and bad news for ISIL.

Beating back the threat that ISIL poses to Iraq is job No. 1 for our Iraqi partners and for our coalition. But even if the government in Baghdad fulfills its responsibilities, it will still face a dire challenge because of events in Syria.

If you recall, the coalition's decision to carry out air strikes in Syria came in response to a request from Iraq for help in defending against ISIL's brazen attack.

To date, we and our Arab partners have conducted over 500 airstrikes in Syria, targeting areas where ISIL has concentrated its fighters and on command and control nodes, finance centers, training camps, and oil refineries. Our objective is to further degrade ISIL's capabilities and to deny it the freedom of movement and resupply it had previously enjoyed.

At the same time, we will continue to build up the capabilities of the moderate opposition. And here I want to thank the members of this committee and many others in Congress who have so strongly supported these efforts. Our goal is to help the moderate forces stabilize areas under their control; defend civilians; empower them to go on the offensive against ISIL; and promote the conditions for a negotiated political transition.

Mr. Chairman, we all know that ISIL is a threat to America's security and interests. It poses an unacceptable danger to our personnel and facilities in Iraq and elsewhere. It seeks to destroy both the short and long term stability of the broader Middle East. And it is exacerbating a refugee crisis that has placed a terrible economic and political burden on our friends and allies in the region.

One thing is certain. ISIL will continue to spread until it is stopped. So there should be no question that we, with our partners, have a moral duty and a profound interest in stopping them.

That is where the fight against ISIL now stands. A coalition that 2½ months ago did not even exist is now taking the fight to the enemy. It was cobbled together by strong American leadership and by steady, intensive diplomacy with countries that disagree on many things, but share an aversion to extremism. I think all of you would agree: we need to summon that same determination to find common ground here in Washington.

That is why, in the hours, days, and weeks to come, we are determined to work with you first and foremost to develop an approach that can generate broad, bipartisan support, while ensuring the President has the flexibility he needs to successfully prosecute this effort.

What do we envision? Importantly—we do not think an AUMF should include a geographic limitation. We don't anticipate conducting operations in countries other than Iraq or Syria. But to the extent that ISIL poses a threat to American interests and personnel in other countries, we would not want an AUMF to constrain our ability to use appropriate force against ISIL in those locations if necessary. In our view, it would be a mistake to advertise to ISIL that there are safe havens for them outside of Iraq and Syria.

On the issue of combat operations: I know that this is hotly debated, with passionate and persuasive arguments on both sides. The President has been clear that his policy is that U.S. military forces will not be deployed to conduct ground combat operations against ISIL. That will be the responsibility of local forces because that is what our local partners and allies want, what is best for preserving our coalition and, most importantly, what is in the best interest of the United States.

However, while we certainly believe this is the soundest policy, and while the President has been clear he's open to clarifications on the use of U.S. combat troops to be outlined in an AUMF, that does not mean we should preemptively bind the hands of the Commander in Chief—or our commanders in the field—in responding to scenarios and contingencies that are impossible to foresee.

Finally, with respect to duration, we can be sure that this confrontation will not be over quickly. We understand, however, the desire of many to avoid a completely open-ended authorization. I note that Chairman Menendez has suggested a 3-year limitation; we support that proposal, subject to provisions for extension that we would be happy to discuss.

To sum up, Mr. Chairman and members of the committee, I ask for your help and support in approving—on a bipartisan basis—an Authorization for Use of Military Force in connection with our campaign and that of our many partners to defeat a terrible and dangerous enemy.

Almost a quarter-century ago, when I was a 47-year-old Senator with a darker head of hair, President George H.W. Bush sent his Secretary of State, James Baker, to ask this committee for the authority to respond militarily to the Iraqi invasion of Kuwait. The country was divided. Congress was divided. But this committee drafted an authorization and it passed the Congress with a majority that the New York Times described as "decisive and bipartisan." Armed with that mandate, Secretary Baker built the coalition that won the first gulf war.

That was a different time and a different conflict that called for a different response. But it was also this body at its bipartisan best—and what we need from you today, to strengthen and unify our own coalition. The world will be watching what we together are willing and able to do. This is obviously not a partisan issue; it is a leadership issue. It is a test of our government's ability and our Nation's ability to stand together. It is a test of our generation's resolve to build a safer and more secure world. I know every one of you wants to defeat ISIL. A bold, bipartisan mandate would strengthen our hand, and I hope we can move closer to that today.

Thank you, and now I would be pleased to respond to any questions you might have.

The CHAIRMAN. Well, thank you, Mr. Secretary. Let me just say there is, I think, undoubtedly, and I will let members express themselves, there is a bold, bipartisan view that we need to defeat ISIL. I think there is no debate about that. Virtually every political element of the spectrum, from those who might be considered dovish to those who might be considered hawkish and everybody in between, I think has a common collective goal of defeating ISIL.

Now, I must say that the administration has not sent us 5, 6 months into this engagement an AUMF. And had the administration sent us an AUMF, maybe we would be better versed as to what the administration seeks or does not seek, and that would be the subject of congressional debate. But that has not happened. And with reference to my distinguished ranking member's comments, you know, if we wait for that and it is not forthcoming by this or any other administration, then the absence of getting an AUMF from the executive branch and Congress not acting because it is waiting for an AUMF from the Executive would, in essence, create a de facto veto of the constitutional prerogative and responsibilities that the Congress has. And so, there are many of us on the committee who in the absence of receiving an AUMF for the purposes of understanding the administration's views felt that it is Congress' responsibility to move forward and define it.

Now, no one has worked harder in the last 2 years as the chairman of this committee to make this a bipartisan effort, not just on that AUMF, but across the spectrum, and I am proud to say that working with the ranking member we have virtually passed out every major piece of legislation on some of the most critical issues on our time from the AUMF, on Syria, and the use of chemical weapons, to OAS reform, to North Korea, to Iran. On a whole host of issues, they have been bipartisan. Virtually every nomination, except, I think, for three of hundreds, have largely been on a bipartisan basis. So there is no one who has driven harder in this process.

But there are some principled views here that may not be reconcilable. And it starts with when the administration itself, and I think you have reiterated what you said earlier in your previous visit here, that the President has been clear that his policy is that the United States military forces will not be deployed to conduct ground combat operations against ISIL, that it will be the responsibility of local forces because that is what our local partners and allies want, what is best for preserving our coalition and, most importantly, what is in the best interests of the United States.

Now, there are those members of the committee and in the Congress who have a much different view than that. They would have a very robust and open-ended use of combat forces in this regard. And if the administration wants that, then it should come forth

and ask for that. But based upon your testimony and based upon
what the President wants, or has said that he wants, I reject the
characterization of my text as something that is constraining to the
President. My text gives the administration the ability to do everything it is doing now and then some.

The text makes clear that activities on the ground for the protection and rescue of members of the U.S. Armed Forces would be allowed; that activities on the ground in support of intelligence col-
lection and sharing would be allowed; that activities on the ground
to enable airstrikes by identifying appropriate targets would be allowed; that activities on the ground that support operational planning would be allowed; and that activities on the ground, including
advice and assistance through forces fighting ISIL in Iraq or Syria,
would be allowed. Obviously airstrikes would be allowed.

So everything that the administration is doing and has said that
it seeks to do and has said, using the President's own words when
he said, which we incorporated into the AUMF when he said—the
President articulated five lines of effort in the campaign to counter
ISIL, including supporting regional military partners, stopping the
flow of foreign fighters, cutting off ISIL's access to financing, ad-
dressing urgent humanitarian needs, and contesting ISIL's mes-
saging.

Nothing in this AUMF constrains the administration or the
President's efforts in any of that regard. Now, indeed authorizing
U.S. ground troops is a subject of debate here, but my text pre-
cludes America from being dragged into another unlimited and
unending war in the Middle East. It does preclude the deployment
of large-scale combat forces, which was done in Iraq, I think, at
great cost and far too great a cost in my view.

So unless I hear something differently, how would you have us
reconcile the view of some members of this committee who want
combat forces to ultimately enter into Iraq and maybe Syria as
well, versus the President's own stated view that that is not what
either we or our allies want?

Secretary KERRY. Well, Mr. Chairman, first of all, let me say I
am not characterizing your bill negatively whatsoever. I think it is
very close to what the President could support, with the exception
of a few of the things that I mentioned, but those are a few. I
mean, you have done a good job of pulling together a broad authorization. And there is a sort of fundamental core that the administration would absolutely support. What I mentioned are a few
things that we think we ought to be able to reconcile with some
work amongst ourselves.

But I think that the President feels, first of all, that with respect
to when and the timing of this, I am here to work with you on behalf of the administration to get this done. And the President has
said all along he wants an AUMF, and there is nothing in the law
that requires the administration to be the initiator of that. And as
I have pointed out to you, there is past record of this committee
taking the lead in drafting it. We are delighted to have your draft,
and we think it is a good draft.

But, as I suggested to you, we believe, number one, in principle
and, number two, in practice in certain situations there are limitations on the choices to the President because none of us can imag-

ine all of the circumstances that may arise. You know, would a hostage attempt have been permitted? What happens if chemical weapons fall into the hands of ISIL, or about to, and there is an emergency need to prevent that from happening because there is a cache that was not reported that we discovered through intelligence?

The CHAIRMAN. The response to that would be an open-ended authorization that would give the President the wherewithal to do any of those and any other things, and, well, not only this President who has 2 years on his term, but whoever would be elected by the American people as the next President of the United States for another year under the authorization as we envision it. And the reason we gave 3 years is because the President himself has said this is a multiyear campaign. We would get past this administration. We would give a year to the new President to come forth and talk about how the war should be prosecuted.

Secretary KERRY. But let me suggest this, Mr. Chairman, because, again, we want to get a broad-based vote. You said some of this may be irreconcilable. You know, I am not sure that it ought to be irreconcilable because the President could not have been more clear about his policy. No one that I know of is in some favor of some open-ended effort, and we have just accepted the idea of the limitation of time with some capacity for review that we ought to work on together so it is sensible. But, you know, it seems to me that there is no way to go through all of the hypotheticals, and you simply wind up tying the hands——

The CHAIRMAN. Well, it sounds to me like you are making a case for a rather open-ended authorization, which if that is what the administration wants, it should say it. But, you know, I would just simply——

Secretary KERRY. No, no, no, absolutely——

The CHAIRMAN. I would simply say to the Secretary that, in fact, the very elements of what the President described as the strategy has been rejected by members, particularly on the other side of the aisle, saying they do not believe that that is a strategy that can succeed. That is a question of debate, but they believe that is not a strategy that can succeed.

Secretary KERRY. Right.

The CHAIRMAN. And they believe, as I am sure you will hear as this unfolds, that there are those members who believe that the only way to achieve with this strategy is to have combat forces and the President having the wherewithal to issue those. So, yes, we cannot imagine every single circumstance, and we think the language has made it sufficiently broad for the President to engage in everything——

Secretary KERRY. Well, here's what——

The CHAIRMAN [continuing]. But the use of long-term combat troops on the ground, which, of course, is totally different than what the President has said.

Secretary KERRY. What I suggest, Mr. Chairman, because I think it is a much better way of trying to resolve this because we are not going to be able to exhaust all hypotheticals and resolve that sort of philosophic debate, is if we sit down very specifically and work through what may be the best balance of this that might be able to bring people from both sides to the table.

The CHAIRMAN. Well, we would—I am always——

Secretary KERRY. The important thing is a broad-based——

The CHAIRMAN. We are always open to that, and, in fact, we have shared several drafts with the White House chief counsel on this issue as we have with the rest of the administration. But to be very honest with you, we get relatively little in response, so if there is a desire to have language that can accomplish the mutual goal, we are certainly willing and open to receive it. But in the absence of it—the absence of language does not—is not going to create a permanent veto of the committee's actions, of the Members of the Senate's actions, and the administration needs to know that. But——

Secretary KERRY. Mr. Chairman, I want you to know 100 percent, President Obama has no intention of sending combat troops in, but he believes, and I believe, and I think all of us share the sense that there is a way to come together to work through how do we resolve this difference in a way that is not open-ended, but I think putting a time limit on it is serious statement about the administration——

The CHAIRMAN. Well, you know, there is a famous movie that says show me the money. I would say show me the language, and maybe we could get there.

Senator Corker.

Secretary KERRY. Well, let us work on it. That is the point.

Senator CORKER. I find this conversation interesting. I would say that I do believe that what the Secretary just said is true, and that is that if we sat down, understood what authority the President, the White House, Secretary of State is seeking, I believe there is a way for us to craft legislation that would be bipartisan, but, more importantly, craft legislation that the administration supports. I mean, passing legislation—passing a bill out of this committee or an authorization is one thing. Passing something on the House and Senate floor is quite another. And the only way that is going to happen is if the administration is firmly behind what we do.

And, again, I would just say to every member here, I think it is harmful to our Nation to begin the process of an authorization and not see it through to the end, and I thought the last effort harmed us greatly. And so, again, I understand the frustration by the chairman. I realize he has tried to have witnesses up here. It has not occurred. But I do believe sitting down with the Secretary and sitting down with the general counsel at the White House as we did last time, I believe that we can come up with authorization that passes the test for the bulk of the members of this committee and actually enacted into law.

Let me ask this question. Do you believe the administration today has the authorities that it needs to carry out the operations that it is carrying out?

Secretary KERRY. Very clearly, yes.

Senator CORKER. So I will say there are some members of this committee that believe otherwise, and believe that the best way we can be effective in making ourselves relevant is just to pass legislation that makes what you are doing legal, and somehow that makes us relevant. That is beyond me. I do not see how that is the case. It seems to me that part of what is missing here is an understanding, so I do not think I am in the place that the chairman characterizes many of the folks on our side of the aisle.

What I would like to understand is how we are going to go about ensuring that we have an outcome here that is worthy of the effort. Again, I go back to what I said in the opening comments. We have had multiple efforts since World War II that just candidly did not end well. They did not produce the outcomes. That is how you made your name in the public world was talking about that. And I would just say that for all of us to conduct a situation where we pass an AUMF, I think it would be good to understand how the administration is going to go about it.

And so, let me ask you this. Is the strategy evolving, yes or no? The strategy of how you are going to go about this evolving.

Secretary KERRY. Well——

Senator CORKER. Are you building—are you building on successes right now to try to more—are we going to go against Assad? Let me just ask you that question since——

Secretary KERRY [continuing]. Well, let me—look——

Senator CORKER. Do we plan to militarily go against Assad?

Secretary KERRY. Not at this moment, no.

Senator CORKER. Do we—do you think——

Secretary KERRY. Can I—let me answer the question a little more fully so you understand. When you say do we plan to go militarily against Assad, do we, the United States, plan at this moment to attack Assad as part of this? No. We are asking——

Senator CORKER. Not as part of this.

Secretary KERRY. We are not asking for—we are asking for an ISIL-oriented authorization.

Senator CORKER. Are you going explicitly ask—are you going to explicitly ask for that?

Secretary KERRY. Let me just finish. But we are heavily engaged, thanks to you and the passage of the $500 million authorization and now the training and equip effort that is—all the ground work is being laid now, in addition to other things that you are aware of, to support those who are engaged in the fight against Assad directly. And many of our coalition partners are particularly focused on the Assad component of the equation. So when I say are we the United States? No, and certainly not as part of this authorization, but as part of the policy. But let me—let me try to help you here a little bit here on this. We——

Senator CORKER. Help me this way. Are you going to ever explicitly seek an authorization from Congress?

Secretary KERRY. We are seeking authorization now with respect to——

Senator CORKER. You are—and if you do not receive that authorization, will you continue the operation? That is an explicit seeking. So are you——

Secretary KERRY. The authorization for what we are doing now in both Iraq and Syria?

Senator CORKER. That is correct.

Secretary KERRY. Absolutely we will continue it because we believe we have full authority under the 2001 AUMF and parts of the 2002. But here is where I want to help if I can.

Senator CORKER. Good.

Secretary KERRY. If Congress passes a new Daesh-specific AUMF, we will support the inclusion of language in the new AUMF that will clarify that the Daesh-specific AUMF rather than the 2001 AUMF is the basis for the use of military force. And I think that will comfort to a lot of people. Number two, we will also support the repeal of the 2002 AUMF as part of an effort to clarify that the ISIL-specific AUMF would be the only source of legitimacy for the use of military force against Daesh. And, therefore, we would live under the confines of what we pass here. And I think that is a pretty, you know, clear and important addition to this discussion.

Senator CORKER. So, do you plan to send us a draft that does these things from which to work off of?

Secretary KERRY. Well, in all fairness, we think that the chairman has a draft, which obviously there are some differences of opinion about parts of it. We have a difference of opinion about part of it. For instance, there is a component which is more of a technical fix which refers to the—includes the forces that are included in—you know, associated forces. And we believe that the fighting alongside language that has been interpreted out of the 2001 AUMF is important to a full explanation of how we can fight this effectively. So there are technical fixes like that. But the fundamental draft that the committee has is a fair starting point, and we propose we work from there.

Senator CORKER. So what you are proposing is that the administration begin to engage more fully with Congress to develop an AUMF using some language that has been drafted, but to edit and change that in such a way that you believe more fully addresses the issue we are talking about. Is that correct?

Secretary KERRY. I am not proposing, Senator. I am here doing it.

Senator CORKER. Okay.

Secretary KERRY. And we are ready to——

Senator CORKER. And so, what do you think would be the appropriate timeframe to work through all of that? I know that many of us would like——

Secretary KERRY. Well, I think over the course of the next days. I mean, let us—I do not think it is going to be finished by Thursday or Friday, but I think that we could engage in this effort over the next days, and as we come back in early January, let us——

Senator CORKER. And do you think it would be helpful——

Secretary KERRY. Believe me, we are anxious to operate with—this helps everybody.

Senator CORKER. Yes, I actually——

Secretary KERRY. This is an important effort for the Congress, an important effort for the country——

Senator CORKER. Other than not explicitly asking for an authorization, to be candid, I very much appreciate what you are saying, and think it is exactly the way we should go about it, and I appreciate you coming up here. I know there are Members on the other side of the aisle that feel very differently about that and feel that we should act this week, and I understand that and appreciate it. I plan to conduct myself in a way, again, that we do not harden ourselves against each other prior to the first of the year when we are a little more closer to the line.

Secretary KERRY. Senator, if we could do it in the next days, we are not trying to not do it.

Senator CORKER. Well, I mean, I think most of us would like to hear from the Pentagon. I mean, you are talking about boots on the ground, and I think that would be a helpful thing to hear about. And I think having some intelligence briefings, and typically, again, we would sit down with the general counsel from the White House and the State Department to work through the language. But I appreciate you coming here.

Secretary KERRY. Thank you. Thank you, Senator.

Senator CORKER. And I understand where we are, and hopefully we will move toward a real bipartisan authorization that most of us can get behind.

The CHAIRMAN. Senator Boxer.

Senator BOXER. Thank you. Secretary Kerry, thank you for the work you do. You know, I believe President Obama has the authority to go after ISIL because I voted to give any President the authority to go after the outgrowth of al-Qaeda, so I feel he has got it. But having said that, this is a threat to humanity that I do not think humankind has seen before, so I am assuming you understand why many of us want to go on record on this.

As a former Senator, can you just understand that, not getting into the details, which I personally think our chairman, working specifically with all of us here, and particularly Senator Kaine, has worked so hard to get something that I think reflects exactly what the President said he wanted. But I will not get into the details with you because, you know what, that is our job to vote. Now, it is your job to do something else, and you do it well, but we have got to do our job.

So I just say from the standpoint of a former Senator, you understand then why so many of us would like to go on record on this threat. Is that correct?

Secretary KERRY. Absolutely, Senator. I have total respect for it, and I understand it, and I welcome it.

Senator BOXER. Right.

Secretary KERRY. The President does, too. I mean, again, I want to——

Senator BOXER. Because let me be clear——

Secretary KERRY. The President wants an AUMF.

Senator BOXER. Well, let me be clear. He may have it from a majority of this committee today, and I am hoping it can be bipartisan. The last time he got it was more of a bipartisan vote, and it had to do with Syria, and this committee acted with our chairman and ranking member. And we set forward an AUMF that had limitations on it, and it had a tremendous impact. We did not wait to talk and talk and talk because we knew that Assad had these chemical weapons, and as a result of our vote, even without it going to the floor—I say to my friend, Senator Corker, even without it going to the floor, it had a salutary effect on what happened.

So I want to talk to you about an amazing hearing I had with Senator Paul this morning about ISIL, about their brutality and their abuses specifically. We had an amazing panel, including a woman who is the only Yazidi Member of Parliament, talk to us about what it is like. And I want to place in the record an article that appeared today in the Daily Beast, and it is taken from sort of a question and answer—it is unbelievable—that answers questions of the recruits as they come into ISIL, or Daesh, or whatever we want to call them. And I will defer to you eventually on what we settle on. But can I put this in the record?

The CHAIRMAN. Without objection.

Senator BOXER. Okay. I am going to give you a sample. These questions are disgusting, so I just want people to not to be upset with me, but I think we cannot, you know, not talk about this. So here is one question: "Can all unbelieving women be taken captive?" Answer: "There is no dispute among the scholars that it is permissible to capture unbelieving women." Question: "Is it permissible to have intercourse with a female captive?" Answer: "It is permissible to have sexual intercourse with a female captive." And then they quote Allah because if you do you are free from blame. Question five: "Is it permissible to have intercourse with a female captive immediately after taking possession [of her]?" Answer: "If she is a virgin, he [her master]"—her master—"can have intercourse with her immediately after taking possession of her. However, if she is not, her uterus must be purified [first]."

This is disgusting garbage. And I will tell you, I understand your desire to put this off, to control it. I need to be on record because of what I am learning. Then they say their "knife will continue the strike the necks of Americans." They will "quench their thirst for American blood." This language is evil. It is vicious. And as Assistant Secretary Tom Malinowski from your administration, said today, when it comes to being terrorists, they are in a league of their own. So, and I know there are—Senator Johnson was there. He asked really good questions, and basically he was making a good point. He said, look, there are so many other groups out there. So he is concerned, and he will speak for himself. But my point is, and I made the point today, I was a kid growing up in the inner city, and if you got the biggest bully on the block, that helped a lot with the rest of the bullies.

So I just want to make a point to you. I have read what our chairman has written. There is a lot of room here for flexibility. Please look at it, Mr. Secretary. I think it is very important.

I did not vote to go to war in Iraq, and I treasure the fact that I voted no. This cannot be boots on the ground, another invasion, and the rest. It cannot be. And if it is, I will not vote for it. But I think what the President is doing, which is to work with others on the ground, particularly, for example, the Kurds, and hopefully we can do it with the Syrian moderates. I know there is a lot of debate about whether there are any moderates left. Some say there are, some say there are not. But I think that we are on the right track here.

And I am sad, frankly, that we have not been able to work with you to craft something together, but I understand you want to do more work. You want to bring in more parties. I have no problem with that. But I just want to say to you, I hope you understand the passion with which everyone that I have talked to views this question. And I hope the administration will not take it as some kind of act of—an unconstitutional act if we go ahead today without you, because if you read the Constitution, it is clear what our responsibilities are.

And I just hope you will take it if we do pass this, and I hope we do, to codify exactly what the President said, that instead of being concerned about it, as I think you are a little concerned about it. Hopefully you can embrace it, and that you can work with us to make it better. But I do not think we should put this off because I am done—I have got to go on record. My constituents expect me to go on record.

The CHAIRMAN. Senator Risch.

Senator RISCH. John—Mr. Secretary, thank you for coming today. We do truly appreciate you coming here to talk to us about this. We have been anxious to do it for some time. So that the record is clear here, you are here in front of us today on behalf of the President of the United States asking for an AUMF, is that correct?

Secretary KERRY. Correct.

Senator RISCH. Okay. Is there a reason this has taken so long?

Secretary KERRY. Well, we asked for an AUMF last time I was here in September, and we are prepared to work and have an AUMF.

Senator RISCH. But this is a different situation now than you were here in September.

Secretary KERRY. I know, but, you know, Senator, I think you have got to look at what has been going on here. Mosul fell 6 months ago tomorrow. And the first thing the President did, and, in fact, we started reacting in January, we took our ISR flights up from 1 a day—from 1 a month to 60 a day way back. We started pouring in additional supplies, and we realized, you know, that we had a different kind of threat. No one quite anticipated the fold that took place in Mosul and so forth and the march toward Baghdad, but since then that has been stopped in its tracks, pushed back.

And the point I am making is that the first step was to get a government in Iraq that you could work with.

Senator RISCH. But I guess——

Secretary KERRY. And so there was a period of months there, and then we got into September, and since then we have said we want an AUMF, and we are prepared to work to do it.

Senator RISCH. Well, you know, this is the first time anybody has come in front of this committee to ask for an AUMF. A letter from the President would have been responded to, and certainly if someone like yourself would have come up here and said, look, this is what we want to do. But I guess what aggravates me about this is, you know, our enemies have got to be looking at this and saying, look at what is going on over there, because this should not be—this is not a Republican-Democrat thing. This really is not a first branch versus the second branch thing, although certainly there are some undertones of that.

But we need to work together on this thing. I am with the chairman on, I guess, feeling aggravated that this thing is playing out like this. We ought to all be pulling the wagon together on this. This is a serious American problem, not a Congress versus President problem, not a Republican-Democrat problem. So you can understand our frustration on this, and admittedly we do have a difference in what the roles are of each party.

The Founding Fathers were very wise when they put in the hands of the first branch of government the power to declare war, and not give it to the second branch, which is the military branch—one of their responsibilities is military. So we take this seriously, and I think the American people take this seriously. It has certainly served us very well over the years. But let me ask this. If Senator Menendez's passes, if his resolution passes, will the President sign that?

Secretary KERRY. Well, I have not asked the President whether he will sign it or not because the President is hopeful that since we generally agree with it, we can work through the differences that do exist. And the President wants to preserve the flexibility that he believes we need, and that is within the prerogative of the President. But he is prepared to work with you to try to see—we are all prepared to work to try to arrive at an understanding of how we can do that.

Senator RISCH. And obviously we have—we have some disagreements in that regard since he—if he believes that the 2001 resolution gives him the authority to do what he is doing now, we have a basic disagreement on that, and that, again, is why I think the Founding Fathers gave us, the first branch of government, the authority to do this. And I guess the question—what would be your opinion as to whether or not the President would sign Senator Menendez's resolution if we pass this this week?

Secretary KERRY. Well, I am not going to, at this point, suggest that I will share with you the advice I will give the President with respect to whether he should veto it or not veto it or what his choices might be if it came to the President. I really think that we are missing the point, though, Senator Risch, if that is sort of the road we go. From the moment I opened my mouth here today I have said to you, and I meant this as does the President, we do not want a bare minimum majority here, and I do not think you want one that way. We need to have a resounding vote in which we are all agreed that we have got the right mix here, and we ought to all be committed to working toward that. I am.

This should not be a, you know, a partisan vote or even an ideologically divided one. I am convinced we can get there. I mean, generally speaking, the chairman's proposal, as I say, has covered a lot of the bases, but we think the President does need some flexibility that is not reflected in it. I think he is owed that constitutionally, though we are not here to make the constitutional argument because we do not want to get trapped into that.

We want to try to get into a place where we find a reasonable way to have the level of flexibility necessary that meets the needs of everybody to know you are not voting for something open-ended, you are not creating a slip—you know, a loophole for the President to do something you do not want him to do. I do not think anybody wants to get into a long-term ground operation here, but we also do not want to hamstring the generals and the commanders in the field and the President who is the Commander in Chief from their ability to be able to make some decision they need to make. And that does not need to take you into a long-standing operation.

Senator RISCH. Let me ask you this. Are you concerned at all about the mechanics of this? I mean, it is highly unlikely we are going to be able to pass an AUMF through both houses during this week. And so, then we are gone until the first of the year. What message do that—are you concerned about the message that that sends?

Secretary KERRY. You know——

Senator RISCH. Because I am with you. I mean, everybody needs to get behind this in one fashion or another and get to express their opinions on it. But here we are now where the request is before us, but it is probably not going to get done. How does that affect things, in your opinion?

Secretary KERRY. To be truthful with you, Senator, I do not believe that that is going to be read as anything except what it is, which is a legitimate process and discussion to get the right end result, and I do not think anybody has any doubt that we are going to get the end result. The fact is that we are going to continue this operation because the President and the administration are absolutely convinced, and I respect your opinion, we have the authority. There is no question about it because the 2001 resolution addressed itself to al-Qaeda, the Taliban, and associated forces. The courts have actually already decided this in the context of our habeas decisions that have been made. So all three branches of government are actually in agreement fundamentally that the 2001 AUMF applies to al-Qaeda.

ISIL, Daesh, you know, again, I prefer Daesh because I know that the Arab world has a real meaning with that, and I think we ought to respect that. But the fact is that they fully understand that we are on the track we are on, and in my judgment, everybody knows that this group merely changed its name. But it was al-Qaeda in Iraq, and it has been al-Qaeda in Iraq from 2004, 2005, and on, and everything it has done is al-Qaeda in Iraq. And there is no question that we authorized this government to go after al-Qaeda wherever they were. And we are doing that in Yemen. We are doing that in Iraq. We are doing that now in Syria, the Khorasan group. Those are all part of the same, and that authorization fits.

But we agree—we have—we have an argument—I mean, there is a nonargument here. We agree with you that it is better to have a new AUMF, and I have come to you and said we will absolutely scuttle the—you know, we would like to refine the 2001 for the period of time we need it, but we will show that this particular authorization is not based on 2001 any longer. It is based on what we are doing here. And that is, I think, a major statement frankly.

Senator RISCH. My time is up. Thank you, Mr. Chairman.

The CHAIRMAN. I would just remind all colleagues that amendments are in order, so if there are those who believe there is a better way to perfect the present text, we certainly can take it up, and consider it, and debate it, and vote on it.

Senator Cardin.

Senator CARDIN. Mr. Secretary, thank you very much. I think your testimony has been extremely helpful, and I thank you for that. There is much more in agreement here than in disagreement. I think there is total agreement that Daesh or ISIL is a barbaric terrorist organization, that we are right in our campaign against them, and that Congress and administration are on the same pages in regards to the legitimate use of force to stop this evil, and to stop its funding, and to stop its ability to cause instability in the region. So we are in agreement on that.

We are also in agreement that Congress and the administration need to work together. We are always stronger when we speak with a united voice. We are now in agreement that we need an authorization for the use of military force that will allow you to continue to conduct the campaign the President has stated that he is doing. I think there is agreement on that. There is agreement on the 2001 and 2002 authorizations—that 2002 needs to be repealed, and 2001 needs to be modified as it relates to Daesh. We are in agreement on that. We are also in agreement with the administration that it should be a time-limited authorization. So I really do think there is a great deal that we agree on, and I thank you. Your testimony has helped us.

But understand that there are some fundamental differences, and I really do think those fundamental differences rest with the separation of powers and the branches of government. I do believe in the War Powers Act. I do believe that Congress has the constitutional responsibility to declare war and to authorize the use of our military forces. I do believe that, and I do believe there have been too many months that have gone by and Congress has a responsibility to weigh in.

So here is, I guess, the point I want to make, and I would love to have your response. The reason why I am so concerned about the language that we put in this authorization being too broad is the explanation you have given that the 2001 authorization clearly authorizes the use of force against Daesh. Let me just read the authorization. I was part of Congress at the time, as several members of this panel were. ''The President is authorized to use all necessary and appropriate force against those nations, organizations, or persons he determines planned, authorized, committed, or aided the terrorist attacks that occurred on September 11, 2001, or harbored such organizations or persons in order to prevent any further attacks and acts of international terrorism against the United States by such nations, organizations, or persons.''

I go through reading that because I think back that if we would have thought after 13 years and after so much of our military battles that were taking place in Afghanistan and Iraq, that this authorization could be used today in the way that it is being used, I think Congress would have drafted different authorization in 2001. So I think it is our responsibility to make sure that we draft this authorization appropriately, recognizing that the President has article 2 powers to deal with the unexpected uncertainties.

If we are going to give you authority to deal with everything we do not know about, then we might as well just repeal the War Powers Act and change the Constitution and give the administration all this power. You can always come back to Congress and seek additional authorization. So I guess I would urge you and would like to get your response as a former member of this committee, former chairman of this committee. Yes, we want to work together. We agree on what we are trying to accomplish, but you must recognize the responsibility that we have in this Congress in the authorizations that we pass, and help us draft an authorization that allows you to do what you need to do. But it will not cover every contingency in the world because that why we meet and we are here, and we can modify authorizations.

So it would be extremely helpful if you could help us with that language—particularly in the two areas that seems like we are in disagreement on geography and contingencies on the use of forces. And I would hope that you would give us further clarification on those two points so that we can be together and speak with a united voice.

Secretary KERRY. Well, Senator, I appreciate and respect your position and your long history of clarity on these kinds of issues in the Senate and the work we did together on these things. But I do disagree with you with respect, and respectfully, that the 2001 AUMF does not authorize this, and let me just tell you why.

I think you know that what happened started in 2001; 2002 you kind of get going with the program; 2002 and 2004 it was continuing. We had, as you know, a Presidential race in 2004 that had a certain debate about this issue. And the fact is that it was in 2004 specifically that ISIL came into our focus and was targeted as what it was, and at that time, Osama bin Laden publicly endorsed the group as the al-Qaeda official affiliate in Iraq. And so, we—you know, had a formal affiliation with al-Qaeda, and that is when we began to take it on. We did take it on. Our troops in Iraq took it on. We were fighting it all of that time. It is a little late to come back and say we did not have the authorization to fight it in 2014 when a whole bunch of folks died fighting it and we put our efforts into it.

Now, they changed their name. Are we going to suggest that any group out there has the right to veto your authorization of use of force because they changed their name? That would be ridiculous. It would give terrorist organizations the right to get out from under just by changing a name. This is the same group. These are the same people with the stamp and imprimatur of support by Osama bin Laden, and we have been fighting them since 2004.

So I do not think there is a question about 2001, but we are actually wasting our time to go back and fight about 2001. Why do I say that? Because, number one, we agree we have to refine it. Number two, we agree we need an AUMF. Number three, we want an AUMF that becomes the exclusive vehicle of authority not relying on——

Senator CARDIN. Yes, I said we agree on that, but where we need help are the two areas where we disagree. I do not want to——

Secretary KERRY. On geographic location you said.

Senator CARDIN. Well, there is no geographic limitation—only one area. Thanks for correcting me. It is just really one area then it seems like.

Secretary KERRY. Right.

Senator CARDIN. I am a little bit confused then. If that is the only area we are in disagreement——

Secretary KERRY. Well, there are two areas that I have singled out. One is in the definition regarding associated forces. We believe that that requires you to make a definition of ideological association or other kind of affiliation, and we believe that gets very complicated, certainly for a commander in the field or for an instant decision about retaliation or so forth. So we want something that encompasses the notion of fighting alongside with, which is the language that has been used in the interpretation of the 2001 AUMF. And that is what we have applied today in our application of force. That is not there. So we wanted the clarity with respect to that, but that is more of a technical fix.

The biggest sort of challenge here is what is the appropriate level of restraint on the President of the United States as Commander in Chief, and Congress' micromanaging of what the military can do and cannot do in the context of its fights. That is all. And none of that should challenge the fundamental prohibition the President has placed on himself that he does not plan to send combat forces in to be part of this battle against Daesh. So I think there is a way here to protect you with some kind of notification perhaps, a requirement.

Senator CARDIN. Just let me point out for the record, a 3-year authorization goes into the next administration, so——

Secretary KERRY. And we thought that was appropriate.

Senator CARDIN. And we agree, but it is important to be very clear about the authorization.

Secretary KERRY. And we thought it was appropriate that it gave whoever is the next President a year to be able to get in place, get all their people in place, make the judgments necessary, but then have some kind of trigger that requires it to be, you know, evaluated in some way. I mean, we are yet to sort of finalize all that. I do not want to do it here now, but let us work on precisely what that ought to be, how it works for both of us so you have a sense that you have got what you need, which is a restraint on the open-endedness, and the President has what he needs is the flexibility to be able to do this properly. And that is a great constitutional balance I think.

The CHAIRMAN. Just for the record, and I think Senator Cardin recognizes this, but since there are others who will be reporting and many who are listening, we have no geographic limitation in the AUMF that we have written. So that, of course, is not an issue.

Senator Rubio.

Senator RUBIO. Thank you, Mr. Chairman. Thank you for being here today, Mr. Secretary. At the outset let me say that I have shared your concern about the release of the CIA report today that was put out by the Senate Intelligence Committee, and I would hope, and I am sure, that the State Department is taking all the appropriate measures to safeguard the security of our personnel in our facilities around the world.

Let me now pivot to the subject of today's hearing. Today you have outlined a pretty clear objective, which I understand that it is to degrade and destroy ISIL and all of the groups that are fighting alongside ISIL. You have also outlined the kind of authorization you would seek, although your point is you do not believe that you require authorization, that you have it existing. You think we act stronger when we have that authorization, and I agree with that point.

You have outlined what that authorization should have it: no geographic limits, which two of the proposals here do not, maybe all three; no intention to use ground troops, but you do not want it ruled out. You agree that at a minimum you do not want to telegraph the limits that we have. And third is, you do not—you do not—well, you are open to a 3-year time constraint. And last, but not least, that it is important that the definition of who the target is be broad enough to encompass affiliated groups or groups fighting alongside ISIL, which I think is critical because of the emergence, for example, of an ISIL associated group in Libya now that is operating in a completely ungoverned space. They do not have Assad to fight. There is no one to fight there. And there is the potential for the emergence of other such groups in North Africa, not to mention the potential for an alliance with the Pakistani Taliban, or the Afghanistan Taliban, or Haqqani network, or any other groups that are in the area.

So here is my question. With such an objective as you have defined today and such a clear idea of what the authorization should look like, I do not understand why the administration has not come forward and presented that as other administrations have done in the past at least as a starting point for this committee to debate, because what happens in the absence of that language is what we have here now—three proposals on behalf of Congress that attempt to micromanage military tactics. And I oppose all three for that purpose.

That is not Congress' role to micromanage military tactics. Congress' role is approve or disapprove of the use of force or to fund or not fund if you do not disagree with it. And the other problem I have with it is that it clearly telegraphs to ISIL, to our enemies, what we will not or will do, where we will do it or where we will not do it, and how long we are going to do it for, which I think also takes a lot of the advantage away from our engagement.

But I blame all of this on the lack of Presidential direction and Presidential leadership. I do not understand why, with such a clear idea about what an authorization should contain, that has not been presented to this committee as far back as September. And here is the other thing that is really problematic. This is a complicated crisis or a complicated conflict. As you have talked about repeatedly today, it involves a coalition, but this coalition includes people that want us to target Assad. Their participation in the coalition is partially because they think it will extend to getting rid of Assad. How does that fit into this equation?

Part of our plan here is to work alongside of moderate rebel elements, but these rebel elements are being bombed by Assad and being attacked by Jabhat al-Nusra, and they may not be around for us to arm and train if they continue to take this beating. How does that fit into this equation? What about the Shia militias? We heard testimony today that these Shia militia are going into non-ISIL communities and attacking Sunnis, burning down their homes, wiping out their neighborhoods. How does that figure into all of this and into Iran's influence there?

And last, but not least, the Kurds and the role they have played, which, by the way, we heard testimony today in Senator Boxer's subcommittee about the role the Kurds have played in providing a safe haven to the Yazidis, and to the Christians, and to other oppressed groups, and they have also been highly effective fighters. All of these complex pieces, and the administration has failed to put together a comprehensive strategy that we can understand about how it all fits together. And for the life of me, I do not understand why with such a clear idea of what the authorization should look like you do not have anyone over there that could type that up real quick and send it over here so we can begin a debate and then amend or work on it.

I think this committee seeks that sort of Presidential leadership on a matter of this magnitude. Certainly previous administrations have drafted such language. There is nothing. And in that vacuum steps in all these proposals because the members of this committee are frustrated at the lack of direction. So I just do not understand when would we see language. Does the White House intend to draft something up and send it to us as a starting point for the sort of discussion that you seek?

Secretary KERRY. Well, Senator, I was around here long enough to know that even if the President sent up some language, there would be just as many bills and just as much debate on what he sent up. So let us not kid each other, I mean, seriously. It is the same debate one way or the other. I mean, if you want to sit there and say, well, the President did not show leadership, the President could say, well, the committee could have begun, drafted it 3 months ago or 2 months ago. I mean, it could go both ways. Let us not get trapped in that.

Senator RUBIO. But the President is the Commander in Chief.

Secretary KERRY. Yes, he is, and he is doing what he is supposed to do, which is putting together a coalition and beginning to win the fight.

Senator RUBIO. But if he wants the authority to win the fight, he has got to tell us what the fight looks like.

Secretary KERRY. Because let me clarify. I made a statement before about, you know, the sole basis that we would make this. What we would make it is the authoritarian current state-of-the-art basis, but as I have also said to you, the President does not need that to have the authority to do what he is doing because he believes, and I believe, and I think constitutional scholars would tell you, he has the authority constitutionally, and he has the authority with respect to the 2001 AUMF, as I have shown you.

But that aside, he is going further to try to provide the precise clarity that you are looking for, and saying that he will put language in here that makes it clear that the AUMF, as passed, will be the designated authority with respect to what we are doing with respect to Daesh.

Senator RUBIO. Well, where is the language?

Secretary KERRY. Well, we have said to you very—I think I have said two or three times today that we think the Senator—the chairman, the Senator from New Jersey has made a strong proposal. I have not come up here and attacked provision after provision after provision. I have said to you we have a couple of differences in it.

They are not incidental. It obviously an important difference this question of what are the limitations, and it is fundamental between the two sides of this dais, I think.

What we are suggesting is we try to work that through in a way that balances it adequately for both sides so we could get the kind of vote that I think could be important. This vote could, in fact, with the proper effort, become the preliminary down payment on what happens subsequently. That would be a good outcome if it were possible.

So my respectful suggestion is in answer to your several comments about the strategy, et cetera, the President has a strategy. General Allen is leading that effort for our coalition in terms of the diplomacy. And GEN Lloyd Austin and CENTCOM are doing an extraordinary job with respect to the military component. But there are other components: the foreign fighters, the humanitarian, the de-legitimization of ISIL with respect to their religious claims, the financing which is being shut down. There are a whole series of broad-based efforts that are underway and in place today.

Senator RUBIO. I know my time has expired. Just for clarity purpose, so the administration's position is that the AUMF they would like to see is the chairman's language with some amendment.

Secretary KERRY. With some changes, that is correct. With some efforts we work on hopefully together to try to work this through.

The CHAIRMAN. Senator Shaheen.

Senator SHAHEEN. Thank you, Mr. Chairman, and thank you, Mr. Secretary, for being here today and for all of your efforts on behalf of this country.

Much of our discussion this afternoon has been around the authority of Congress versus the authority of the President. But I would suggest that this debate is important for another reason because I think this debate is also about the right of the American people, the people that we all represent, to know what is entailed in this country's use of military force against ISIL, including the scope and duration of that. And one of the things that has been said here this afternoon is that we weaken our country rather than strengthen it when we begin a process, like the discussion we are having today, that we know cannot be concluded.

I would actually argue the opposite, and that is that this debate strengthens our resolve in this country, and that our enemies looking at the debate should not be confused and assume that this is weakness that we are having these debates, but rather it is one of the things that makes this country so strong, our ability to debate issues of war and peace. It is part of what our democracy is about.

You said, and I think several of us have agreed with this, that if the committee worked with the White House and understood what the administration wants, that we could probably craft language with some back and forth that we could all agree to, or at least the majority of the committee—a bipartisan majority could agree to. I certainly agree with that. And we have talked about a process in the committee that would have this hearing today, have some time this week to actually discuss it among ourselves. And we were hoping to work with some members of the administration in a classified setting to hear more about what is currently underway with respect to the war against ISIL.

So I guess I would say to you if we are all committed to having that kind of discussion about what should go in the AUMF, should we assume that there are members from the Department of Defense and from the intelligence communities who could also be part of working with us on that kind of a back and forth? And is that something that we could get set, because my understanding is that one of the challenges has been a commitment from folks to actually come and answer some of the questions and the concerns that this committee has had.

Secretary KERRY. I cannot imagine why that cannot be worked out. I mean, I do not know what the schedules are. I know Secretary Hagel was not available because he was overseas, I think in Iraq and elsewhere. So that availability obviously was challenged. But I am confident—I cannot imagine that—you know, as I have said, the administration is prepared to work with you, and we will work out the schedules and see what is doable.

Senator SHAHEEN. Well, thank you. I think that would be very helpful as we are talking about trying to get something that can be garner bipartisan support.

Secretary KERRY. And I understand the desire obviously to hear from the intel and hear from the, you know, DOD.

Senator SHAHEEN. Well, I appreciate that. I think it is very important for us to have this debate, for the committee to act and to work with the administration and see if we can find acceptable language. But to do it in a way that is not open-ended so that we are not, as the committee has said in the past, waiting indefinitely for language that may never come from this administration.

So let me ask some specific questions relative to what is going on with the current operations of our fight against ISIL, recognizing that you may or may not be able to answer some of these questions. But can you talk about the moderate opposition at this point relative to the Syrian regime and the extremists? And there have been a number of reports that that opposition has—is in the process of totally collapsing. Is there any intention to expedite the training and assistance efforts to the moderate Syrian opposition groups?

Secretary KERRY. The answer is, "Yes," there is a great deal of effort to try to expedite at this point in time. The opposition in the south is actually doing fairly well right now, and it is a problem for the Assad regime. But a lot of the fight that is so critical is in the north, and there Aleppo is a challenge, and it is one that we are very, very well aware of. We are working with the Turks right now, having long discussions in order to work through a number of different thoughts about how best to deal with that. There is ISIL up there, there is al-Nusra up there, Jabhat al-Nusra, and the opposition, and then you have the regime.

And so, the President is considering a number of different options with respect to the north, but we are working through those details. General Allen was over there recently meeting with the Turks at some length of discussion about trying to focus in and narrow down who could do what how and so forth. But it is all on a fast track because everybody understands the opposition there is challenged.

Regrettably, a couple of different opposition groups, and there are a number of different opposition groups, did not fare well in their battles, and some—one or two of them actually sort of folded into al-Nusra, which is disturbing and something that folks are looking at carefully. But by and large they have survived. They are holding on. They have been the entity that has been fighting for almost four years now, and we are increasingly doing a number of things to try to make a difference, some of which we cannot lay out here in this committee in open session, some of which are a part of the training effort that we want to get underway.

And happily, the Turkish base for that training and the Jordanian base for that training are complete and ready, and we are starting to get, you know, that moving. We still have to get more going with respect to—Kuwait is only in the beginning stages, and the Saudi training component needs additional infrastructure work, et cetera, in order to be ready.

But believe me it is very, very important to get a number of things in place as rapidly as possible because while they are doing well in the south, the north is a challenge.

Senator SHAHEEN. Thank you. My time has expired.

The CHAIRMAN. Before I turn to Senator Johnson, I do not want there to be any impression here by members of the committee that we have not tried to engage with the administration and solicit and elicit both opinions and witnesses. To the Secretary's credit, he is the one person that has been here on several occasions, and we appreciate that, and I am convinced that as part of his history here, he recognizes the importance of that.

And he has made himself available, although I do not feel that he has the wherewithal to talk about every dimension of this, no matter how well versed he is or how well he has tried. There are intelligence questions here, there are military questions here, but this is what we have.

Now, for timeline purposes, let us understand that the first War Powers notification came to us in June, in June. And then we had the Secretary appear here on September 17 to testify on the anti-ISIL strategy. Then on September 23, we had War Powers notification, making it very clear that this would be a multiyear effort, September 23. And then on November 5, the President actually went before Congress and requested authorization for military operations against ISIL.

So going back to that period of time, this committee, and certainly the Chair, has engaged the administration going back to October when staff had conversations, when we met with the White House counsel to go over a draft of language. And in fairness, we just did not get specificity of responses. So when we talk about "let us work together," there has been an effort to try to achieve exactly that.

I do not want anybody here to think that there has not been an effort or for the public to think, wow, it seems that they are doing Rambo here by themselves. There has been an effort here. And the fact is that requests were made for this hearing, as well as for classified hearings, for others beyond the Secretary to be able to further inform. Those were not—for whatever reasons, logistics, whatever, travel, were not being able to be pursued. So based on the

Senator's questions, I do not want anybody to think here that that effort has not been made.

Senator Johnson.

Senator JOHNSON. Thank you, Mr. Chairman. Mr. Secretary, I just want to pick up a little bit on what the chairman was talking about, the efforts this committee has made. I remember our hearing on May 21 where we had the counsel from the Department of Defense and the counsel from the Department of State. We talked about an authorization for use of military force, and at that point the administration was saying they wanted to engage with the Congress. And then later on, I think July 23, a number of us did go down to the White House, to the counsel's office, and we discussed that authorization.

I recall is two things from that meeting: that the White House counsel was finding a somewhat tenuous connection to previous authorizations, and so they were looking and interested in having a new authorization. I think I left that meeting with the impression that the ball was in the administration's court to draft something, and that is my question.

After all that time, why? Just simply why has the administration not sent us a draft proposal, because it has really been pretty much the history of previous Presidents. I would think that would make sense that the Commander in Chief would like to lay on the table an authorization that he would want to pursue with the actions that he believes are necessary to keep this Nation safe. Why has the President not given us the draft? It would have cleared up so much confusion. So I just simply ask—answer the question, why?

Secretary KERRY. Well, as I have said, I think we have a pretty good draft.

Senator JOHNSON. No. Why has the President not sent a draft? Why did he not write it up himself, or you, or his Secretary of Defense?

Secretary KERRY. It is my understanding there have been about seven meetings, and I do not know. I was not present in any of those meetings, but the seven meetings have discussed the draft. The chairman himself said they went and talked about the draft. There is not requirement for the President to send it up.

Senator JOHNSON. But would it not make it a lot—okay.

Secretary KERRY. I do not know if it, but as I said earlier to Senator Rubio, would it have made life easier? Would it have changed the debate? It is the same debate. You have language in front of us which we are now working with, and the President has said that by and large it is pretty good. This is not the first time that the committee has exerted leadership to put language together that the President has asked for and welcomed.

Senator JOHNSON. Again, I will not get an answer. That is fine. The reason I think we need to review past authorizations is because I think there are legitimate differences to whether or not, for example, the 2001 authorization really does apply right now. Let me read why. It is all past tense. It is talking about nations, organizations, persons he determined, planned, authorized, committed, or harbored. Those are all past tense. There is nothing in here talking about associated forces. It is kind of describing them.

But there is legitimate concern about whether or not that actually does authorize its current use. And, again, my understanding in the White House, they seemed also to be grappling with the tenuous connection between the current use of military force and that authorization. But I want to go back a little bit further because I think exploring this language and exploring the history makes sense.

In World War I and World War II, we actually had a total of two declarations of war in World War I and six in World War II, the authorizations were pretty open-ended. They gave the President the authority he needed to defeat the enemy. In World War I, it was a declaration of war against Germany, and this is what the authorization said: ''to bring the conflict to a successful termination.'' And even in the 2001 authorizations, the President was authorized to use ''all necessary and appropriate force.'' That is what past Presidents wanted in terms of authorization, the authority to be Commander in Chief and to accomplish the goal.

Here is my question. Has President Obama deviated from the goal he stated to degrade and ultimately defeat ISIS?

Secretary KERRY. Not in the least.

Senator JOHNSON. What is the goal of this process then? I mean, is it to have a bipartisan authorization? Is it to have members be able to put themselves on the record, or is it to produce an authorization that gives the President the congressional authority to actually accomplish that goal?

Secretary KERRY. Well, it is obvious. Senator, the purpose of the AUMF is to authorize in its new and modern context, its state-of-the-art context, the challenge that we now face with a very different kind of extended threat, if you will. And I think the discomfort that has been exhibited on both sides of the aisle with the reliance on 2001, which we believe absolutely withstands any judicial scrutiny whatsoever and is legitimate. But the discomfort that exists should be clarified. And the American people, the President believes, are owed a 2014 commitment, not a 2001 commitment.

Senator JOHNSON. I completely agree, and the other thing the American people are owed is for the President to draft what that authorization should look like so we have something to work from. What I would argue as well is that we need an authorization because this is a different kind of enemy. This is not a nation-state that is going to be pretty obvious what it is going to look like when they are defeated. We need to have a discussion about what defeat looks like. We need to define that term.

I would also argue what we need is we need an authorization that is good not only for President Obama, but a future President, because I agree with President Obama: this is not going to be a war or a conflict that ends quickly. So that is why I am looking to the Commander in Chief, I am looking for what he believes he needs and what his successor or successors might need to grapple with and take the actions they need to take to keep this Nation safe with this brand new—over the last decade or two—this brand new threat, not a nation-state, but an ideology that wants to kill Americans.

Secretary KERRY. The President would agree we should, and that is exactly what we are trying to do.

Senator JOHNSON. Well, again, I will look forward to the draft because it would make this process just a whole lot easier.

Secretary KERRY. Well, again, we are pretty close as we are sitting here. I think we just have to sit down and work through the differences. The President has said that in general terms this is a pretty good——

Senator JOHNSON. Does the President really believe that ISIS or the new name, Daesh, will be defeated in 3 years? Does he really believe that is the case?

Secretary KERRY. No, the President has said this is going to take a long time.

Senator JOHNSON. Why would we limit ourselves to a 3-year time period then? Why would you want to hamstring his successor having to come back before—I am sorry—this dysfunctional body? Let us face it. We had this hearing in May of this year, and now we are back here in December. This is not going to be concluded with authorization for the use of military force. We will take a show vote, but this will not give President Obama the authority that he needs and that his successors will need. Why would he even agree to a 3-year limitation? Is that a responsible thing for a President to do?

Secretary KERRY. Well, Senator, first of all, look, it is hard to have the argument both ways the way you are trying. If it is dysfunctional, maybe then there is a real reason why the President did not send it up. I think that is not the reason, and I do not mean to make fun of it. He is not—that is not the reason, and that is not where it is. The President—for 2½ months now we have been preoccupied in trying to focus on putting together the strategy, implementing the strategy, building the coalition, and doing what we have needed to do. There have been seven meetings during that time. I do not know what happened at those meetings, but there have been seven meetings.

Senator JOHNSON. Well, let me ask you. Why not?

Secretary KERRY. Well, let me just—let me just——

Senator JOHNSON. Why are you not aware of what happened in those seven meetings?

Secretary KERRY. Because I am not in those meetings. Those are in the White House. That is White House counsel. I work——

Senator JOHNSON. They are not giving you a briefing or sending you a memo?

Secretary KERRY. I think, Senator, let me just come to your other question, which I believe was—you asked about the timeframe, would we limit it? Why would we limit it? And if you listened carefully, what I said is I am not in favor of that limitation without the ability to have the renewal. But I am trying to balance.

Look, what we are trying to do here, I think all of us—let us not get dragged down into a sort of, you know, unnecessary debate here. We want to build the strongest vote possible. We want to see if we can meld the differences into something that is acceptable to both sides. That has often happened here historically, and certainly when I was here in 1991 and other times when we did this, we did that. We ought to be able to do it now. There is a balance of interests.

Now, some people have an interest in protecting the complete open-endedness of the Presidential authority as they deem it to be given under the Constitution, and there are others here who, by virtue of experience and, you know, bad experience, want to have a little restraint, and they are trying to balance. We think we are offering a way to try to figure out how you do that, which is to give a sort of fixed period of time during which you will have the chance, the Congress, to take stock of it so it is not purely open-ended, but also so it is a responsible process that I will not end unnecessarily. There will be a review of some kind, and that is what we ought to sit down and work out.

How does that work? What is the appropriate way to do that? What is the trigger, so that there is a respectful assessment of where we are, what is happening, of how it has been implemented, and that it is not, in fact, open-ended and dangerous and dragging us on into an open-ended ''war.'' So I think that is what we are trying to balance. A lot of that comes out of the experience of Iraq or even Afghanistan. People are worried about it. They do not want it to be that again, and everybody is sensitive to that. So I think we are just trying to find the appropriate balance between those things, and I think, as I say, the chairman's mark is a good starting place, and we should work off of that.

The CHAIRMAN. Senator Coons.

Senator JOHNSON. Thank you, Mr. Secretary.

Senator COONS. Thank you, Chairman Menendez, and thank you, Ranking Member Corker. And thank you, Secretary Kerry.

Secretary KERRY. I would think you would have an administration say the chairman's mark is a good starting place. It does not happen that often.

Senator COONS. Thank you, Secretary Kerry, and thank you for your hard work and your leadership in assembling and helping steer the coalition against ISIL. And thank you for your presence with us today. I am relieved we are having this debate and that we are having it in the open. I believe the American people deserve, and our values demand, exactly this sort of a robust and open debate, and I think that Congress should not adjourn until we vote on an AUMF.

We have raised important and difficult issues, and as you, Mr. Secretary, just commented, it is in large part because of the difficult history of the lessons learned from the cost, and the reach, and the scope, and the complexity of our conflicts in Iraq and Afghanistan, and the 2001 and 2002 authorizations that were the foundation in some ways of those actions that there are real concerns here. And I think this is the sort of debate, the sort of give and take between executive and legislative branches that our Founders imagined. We have to, in many way, reexamine and reset that relationship.

Let me also just put on the table, I think, an important issue that has not been touched on so far, an issue that is vitally important not just for this committee, but for Congress to consider. The wars in Iraq and Afghanistan, according to a CRS report that just came out, there was a total of about $1.69 trillion requested to pay for the cost of those two wars. And as other members have commented, the Congress has two ways to restrain the Executive in the conduct of long wars. First, the authorization or declaration of war, and second, how we fund them. And it is my hope, my expectation, that we cannot write another blank check for war, as was unfortunately the case under previous Presidents and previous Congresses for previous conflicts.

Now, paying for war is not fiscally, but also morally responsible. It is not right to expect that the only people who sacrifice would be our troops and their families. And so, expressly having a conversation about how to offset the cost of this war through a reduction in spending or an increase in revenue or both will help Americans have a more direct connection to the conflict and an awareness of its impact, not just in terms of our spending, but our steadily growing national debt.

I am aware this responsibility does not fall just on this committee, but it is the duty of the Congress, as we debate the scope and the strategy for this conflict, to also look squarely at its cost and how to pay for it. And so, I will continue to raise that issue as we move forward with the debate about the AUMF.

Let me, Secretary Kerry, if I might, first just bear down on an issue that I do not think I have heard a clear and concise answer to. So, if we are trying to come up with an AUMF that recognizes some of the challenges of the 2002 AUMF and that puts some restraint on the use of ground troops, and that strikes you as unacceptable in this effort, as you put it, to balance restraint against an open-ended conflict while allowing the President, the Commander in Chief, the flexibility to prosecute this conflict successfully. I think one of the reasons there remains real hesitation, real resistance to just an open-ended commitment to conduct of any kind is that we have not had a full debate or discussion about the strategy. We cannot go home and clearly defend what the strategy is, although you laid out the five core areas in which there is ongoing and effective activity.

Could you accept an AUMF that was limited in time, as you discussed previously, and that initially had a limitation on large-scale ground combat, but required and examination of strategy and then a reconsideration of the AUMF to remove that limitation on the Commander in Chief's scope to conduct this and prosecute this war?

Secretary KERRY. Well, I think by implication the way the administration is looking at it, there is some restraint because the President has been pretty clear. And there is no current scenario that he would imagine where—I mean, if you are putting a restraint in time, you are automatically not getting into a long-term activity. So the 3 years is, in fact, the best automatic limitation on this problem of long term.

And if you have the right kind of formula for the trigger or for the—you know, I can think of several now, but I am not going to go into them now. I do not think it is appropriate to do that here, but we could—you know, we could certainly sit down and bang out the ways that balance the interests that create a sufficient level of review so you are certain you are going to get your whack at it, but it is not—you know, it is not self-limiting so that the wrong message is sent, and you are not going to prosecute the war. You know, some people still have—struggle with that terminology. But that is where I think it is.

So I would suggest there is a balance, and I think we can work that out. I do not think you have to have the ground troop limitation by virtue of the 3-year piece.

Senator COONS. Well, Mr. Secretary, I join many of my colleagues in both expressing a desire for a bipartisan AUMF, and for a more robust and more broad discussion and debate about the strategy and what the direction is going to be. But I do want to make it clear that I support the conduct of this conflict against ISIL, that I think they are a real and present threat to the United States and our allies in the region, and I do think we should be supporting our armed forces. But weeks have turned into months since the War Powers notifications came up here, and I think this Congress needs to be more actively engaged in being accountable for authorizing this conduct.

Let me move to one more question with the time I have. It was announced today roughly 1,500 soldiers from the international coalition against ISIL will join roughly 3,100 Americans in the train and equip mission in Iraq to train the Peshmerga and the ISF. How else will our coalition partners assist in the campaign? In a previous conflict in the region, many of our partners contributed significantly to the financial cost of the operations. Will we be complementing this training role with financial contributions from our allies and partners, and can you give us any further update on your expectations around ground troops? I was encouraged by your comment that many of our allies and the administration believe that non-U.S. ground troops are mostly likely to be effective in this conflict and in this context.

Secretary KERRY. Well, the answer, Senator, is that—the answer is, ''Yes,'' a number of countries are committed to providing financial input as well. To some degree, some of them, it depends what we choose to do. But the answer is, yes, they are prepared to provide financial assistance, and already are in some ways. For instance, the training facilities in some of their territory they are taking of.

In addition to that, there will be a variance between countries as to who is doing what. As you know, five Arab nations are flying with us in the missions over Syria—Saudi Arabia, United Arab Emirates, Bahrain, Jordan, and Qatar. And in addition to those five, we have countries from all over the world who are contributing one way or the other, whether it is to training, providing direct assistance, providing humanitarian assistance, providing equipment, providing arms, and, in some cases, presence on the ground in the case of a number of our close allies in the actual training activities. Australia is a case and example, Great Britain, others are doing that. So there is a full-fledged, broad-based engagement by many different countries in many different activities.

Senator COONS. Thank you, Mr. Secretary. Thank you, Mr. Chairman.

The CHAIRMAN. Senator Flake.

Senator FLAKE. Thank you, and thank you for being here, Mr. Secretary. You are a very good diplomat. You have mentioned that the President does not need to outline his AUMF because we have one here, the chairman's mark. But then in your testimony you very clearly state, pretty clearly at least, diplomatically that we need to do far better than that.

And Senator Johnson went through some of the AUMFs that we had or those facsimiles from World War II. If you go beyond that, I am looking at a few of them here. The one in 1955 with regard to defense of Taiwan, the President "authorized to employ the armed forces as he deems necessary." In 1957 in the Middle East, "authorized to cooperate with and assist any nation or group of nations." 1964, Southeast Asia, "take all necessary measures to repell any armed attack." Then we come to this one where the President is authorized "subject to the limitations in subsection (c)."

I would submit that that is not very comforting to our allies, and it is not a very strong AUMF. In fact, it more accurately may be an authorization for the use of not too much military force. When you signal to our enemies and to our allies that we are not going to use ground troops, and we certainly do not want to. We may not anticipate that we will. But to put that aside and say we are not going to just does not strike me as wise.

The President as Commander in Chief can certainly have that policy, but he can change his mind as conditions warrant. It is far more difficult once the Congress has spoken to go back to the Congress and say now conditions have changed on the ground, and we need a new AUMF. What do your enemies do in the meantime? What do our allies do in the meantime?

So I would respectfully say that when my colleagues here are saying that the President needs to show more leadership and actually put an AUMF together and present it to the Congress, one that is in keeping with the history and what we need for the future. All of us can draft our own. I have drafted mine. I will be glad to give you a copy. But that does not substitute for one that will come from the President and for him to make the strong case to Congress that this is what we need. That is what we need. As you put it, our allies deserve it. They need it. Our enemies need to understand it, and we need this country together.

So, again, I would ask you why in this context can we not get the President to submit his AUMF. And all due respect to the chairman and others who have tried to put something together here that can pass, I would submit that it is not worth it to get something that so limits our President in his options, that it is not comforting to our allies, and it is too comforting to our enemies.

Secretary KERRY. Well, Senator, thank you for your comments. Listen, I said at the outset that the problem that the President and the administration has with this is this question of the limitations and restrictions, so, I mean, I have been very clear. But I have also said we think there is a way to try to work with you. We do not want to, you know, sit here and stop all capacity to be able to get a strong resolution by simply being stuck in a place where we say that, you know, we are not going to accept any kind of appropriate calibration of this. So we think that there is a way to try to figure that out.

Now, I do not disagree with you. I do not want your second example—what was the second one you said about the prior use of force authorizations? You went back to the fifties?

Senator FLAKE. It was something in 1957, the Middle East.

Secretary KERRY. Yes, 1957, Middle East, yes. Well, certainly at least from '64, which Senator McCain and I are pretty familiar with, onto Iraq and others, I think there has been a strong reaction in the country that unfettered openness has resulted in some bad judgments that have cost the country an awful lot of money and other assets. And I think that the tension here in this debate obviously is between those who are willing to provide that full constitutional authority that the President can make those decisions and should not have any restraint at all, with those who are cautioned by the past and want to have some adequate congressional restraint, reflecting the reluctance of the American people to get into another open-ended deal.

Senator FLAKE. I would say——

Secretary KERRY. So how do you balance that? And I think there is a way to balance that. Part of the balance comes in this 3-year duration notion with Congress' preordained and defined input. It seems to me that is a pretty measured way to try to do it. Now, maybe there is some other notification requirement that we could work through here and so forth.

I do think, and the President feels, and I know that the members of the military feel very strongly, that in terms of actually implementing—I mean, we all have decided we have got to defeat these guys. Everybody is agreed that we have to degrade and defeat ISIL. And I do not think that Congress is going to sit here and say that, well, we are going to tell you exactly step for step how you are going to do that. That is what we have the professional military for.

Senator FLAKE. If I may——

Secretary KERRY. And we need to make sure that, you know, there is a balance here between the President's rights as Commander in Chief and the military's ability to implement and achieve our goal. That is the balance we are looking for.

Senator FLAKE. I would say post-1964, you mentioned there has been an attempt to balance this because of some situations we have had. Those have been more on—any conditions that have been with the AUMF has been on the—we can only authorize the use of force after all diplomatic measures have been exhausted. That is typically what is done on the front end, but once we commit ground troops, or our military forces, I should say, then in virtually every case that I have seen, unless I am not aware of others, we have never tied the President's hands or, as you put in here, that we do not preemptively bind the hands of the Commander in Chief. And I just do not think it would be wise to do so here. And so, thank you for your testimony.

Secretary KERRY. Thank you very much, Senator. Appreciate it.

The CHAIRMAN. Senator Udall.

Senator UDALL. Thank you, Mr. Chairman. Thank you, Senator Menendez, and thank you, Secretary Kerry. Senator Menendez, you really pushed to get us here to this point. I mean, and I know the ranking member did, too, and so that is important. And, Secretary Kerry, we would not be here without you because we needed at least one witness to try to address this, and I really appreciate you helping us work through it.

I have a couple of questions just about how things are going now. Maybe you cannot answer them. The success of our United States strategy in Iraq appears predicated on the shift of Sunnis away from the Islamic State and toward cooperation with the government. And to what extent is that shift occurring, if at all, right now, and what factors will determine the extent of the alteration in allegiances?

Secretary KERRY. Well, that is a very good question and an appropriate one because essential to the ability to be able to be successful in Iraq will be inclusivity of the Sunni population, the commitment of the Sunni tribes, the tribal leaders to take on this fight, and to ultimately join with the national army in order to push ISIL out. That, I believe, is a work in progress. Not "I believe." That is a work in progress.

There are currently a number of battalions that are in training. You know, those battalions as they move out of training will allow those that are experienced and held together to go out into the field. There is work being done with the tribal leaders right now. The tribes—a certain number of people that are coming together to provide a Sunni fighting force as part of it. There is a plan to be implemented to put in place a national guard which will be more reflective of people and where they live so that there is an inherent investment by them in defending that community, which there did not exist in previous——

Senator UDALL. Is the shift taking place, and to what extent? That is what I really want to get at the heart of.

Secretary KERRY. That shift is beginning to take place. It is beginning to take place. It is in its early stage. I do not want to promise you something that is beyond where it is, but it is beginning, and it is legitimate, and there have been successes. The Baiji area has been—the refinery has been—you know, it is not complete yet, but it has been a success thus far in pushing ISIL back. The Amirli relief effort that took place. The Mosul—the Haditha Dam, the Mosul Dam. These are areas where there have been clear successes. And there are increasing other efforts that are taking place.

So we believe that there are very promising signs. It is too early to stand up and down and shout, but it is moving in the right direction. And we feel confident that it is the right strategy.

Senator UDALL. Now, when we announced that we were going to—when the President announced degrade and destroy ISIL, a number of groups around the world in Islamic countries pledged allegiance to the Islamic State. How should the authorization of force treat groups who have pledged their allegiance to the Islamic State, including, as of December 2014, groups in Algeria, Libya, Egypt, Yemen, and Saudi Arabia?

Secretary KERRY. They should be associated forces. They fit under that category.

Senator UDALL. So they—okay. Now, and you have outlined here the three areas of authorization of force. One of them is duration. And you mentioned in your testimony, Secretary Kerry, a provision that provides for an extension under certain circumstances. So you are willing to go with 3 years, and just as an aside I am much closer to Senator Paul with 1 year. But assuming you are willing to go with the 3 years, who is the extension the choice of? Is it the administration or the Congress, or do you want a provision that just allows the administration under specific circumstances to go forward?

Secretary KERRY. Well, that is where it has to be—I mean, that is the precision of the language that we have to sit down and work through. And I would want White House counsel and others obviously to weight in very heavily on that.

Senator UDALL. But this is a policy question.

Secretary KERRY. Well, it is always policy question. Congress always has the ability to cut off money for something.

Senator UDALL. Right.

Secretary KERRY. I mean, you have the power of the purse no matter what is stated, and the President has the power of the Commander in Chief and Executive authority. And he will make his decision, and that is the debate. My thought is that if you sit down and work this through, you will come up with an equation that works effectively.

Senator UDALL. But you will not today say that provision should be Congress revisiting it at 3 years or the administration——

Secretary KERRY. Well, I think the administration deserves first crack. There is no question about that, but it ought to be done in a way——

Senator UDALL. So it is not a real 3 years. You want a longer duration.

Secretary KERRY. No, I said first crack at it. I mean, I do not think Congress is going to sit here and say, yes, you ought to continue it, and the Executive is saying I am not going to order my troops to do that. Clearly the Chief Executive, Commander in Chief, is going to make a decision as a matter of the administration's foreign policy and its war fighting policy. But there needs to be, obviously I would assume for you, some manner of weighing in on that. And how that is effected and what the language is is precisely what we ought to be working through. That is not for me to casually throw it out here this afternoon, and I think that would be, you know, inappropriate. But I know there is a way to balance this.

Senator UDALL. And I think the important thing is that Congress, whatever the period of time, needs to reweigh back in, be involved, be engaged in terms of where we are at that particular point. And in the three areas you outlined on the authorization of force, my opinion is what we are talking about is an open-ended authorization. There is no geographic limitation. I think there should be geographic limitation. I do not think we should allow the administration to go into Libya or a number of other countries surrounding this area.

Secondly, this language "no boots on the ground," the President has used that language very specifically over and over again. That should be in the resolution. It should be strong. And if you want to have boots on the ground, you should come back to the Congress in order to continue with a war with American troops on the ground.

And as far as the duration, I mentioned that earlier. I think one year would be more appropriate because it has been very difficult for us to get the information we need in order to find out whether we should be moving forward or not. And then just as a final issue here, I want to mention the issue of paying for this. There is no doubt that we are starting a third war in this particular region. You do not have to look very far to know that it is a war to look at Kobani, look at the troops that are fighting, look at the air strikes.

And one of the biggest questions with all wars is how do you pay for them, and up until Iraq and Afghanistan, the generation that fought a war paid for the war. And I believe we started a policy, which was a very misguided policy. We put Afghanistan, we put Iraq, we put them on the credit card. So as the President prepared to present a plan to the Congress to pay for this war, the President says it is going to be lengthy. It is going to be 3 years. Is he willing to put forward war bonds, war surcharge, a terrorism tax like some have called for? Is he willing to put anything on the table in order to pay for this?

Secretary KERRY. Well, the President has put on the table—the request for $1.52 billion was additional resources for the Department of State/USAID to degrade and ultimately defeat ISIL. We have put additional funding requests in. There is $520 million for-eign——

Senator UDALL. I am talking about paying for it with a war—like all the other wars that have been paid for, not putting——

Secretary KERRY. Well, this is paid for within the context of the current budget and the process.

Senator UDALL. Well, I take it—I take it you are not——

Secretary KERRY. And that is what we are doing. But in addition to that, let me just say one thing, though, Senator, if I may. Look, I respect the notion that you have an opinion about 1 year and strong feelings about—you know, strong feelings about the geographic area, et cetera. But I will say to you, if you limit this geographically, you are saying to—and we did not limit al-Qaeda geographically. And we have been able to do very real damage to al-Qaeda and keep plots from hitting us—the Christmas bombing plot, other plots that have come out of other places than Pakistan or Afghanistan. And I think one of them came out of Yemen, another out of another location, Northern Africa.

I mean, we have been able to do those things because we are not limited by geographic authority. And I will tell you that we would have a much bigger problem today if we were, and it would be terrible to send a message to these guys, you have a safe haven over here and safe haven over here. And if we do not take this seriously—I mean, this is bigger than just where it is in Iraq and Syria.

Senator UDALL. I know——

Secretary KERRY. And secondly, let me crystal clear. We did not start this. We are not about to start a third war. Osama bin Laden started this on 9/11/2001, and he has continued it in absentia obviously through what al-Qaeda does. ISIL, Daesh, is an extension of al-Qaeda. It is part of the same thing. It is clear what they want to do, and it is a risk and danger to all of the region, which is why we have this extraordinary coalition.

This is not the United States of America trying to start something, and there is not a country in the region that is not looking to us for leadership right now and working with us and grateful for what we are doing here, because they are at risk—Saudi Arabia, Egypt, the region, Syria, Israel. You run the list—Jordan. Ask any of them. That is why they have publicly stepped up and they are part of this effort.

So I think we have to understand this is the fight of the generation. That is what I believe certainly, and President Obama believes it. And we need to understand what a big challenge it is, and it is going to take a lot more than just trying to deal with it through this military component. There is no ultimate military solution, though we have to fight back, against the Daesh. But if a lot of young kids out there are left to their own devices and do not have options for jobs, and education, and a decent life, and opportunity, and respect, and dignity, and so forth, this is going to continue. And the United States and our allies need to work at that side of the ledger also.

The CHAIRMAN. Senator——

Senator UDALL. Well, that is something that we can agree on, and I know my time is up. Thank you, Mr. Chairman.

The CHAIRMAN. Senator McCain.

Senator McCAIN. Well, let me say I agree with your comments about the parameters of an AUMF, but, you know, this is really kind of a charade we are going through because the Congress of the United States is not going to act in the next couple of days, because I have been involved in many AUMFs, and not a single one was generated from the Congress.

The reason why the Constitution calls the President the Commander in Chief is because he is supposed to lead, and if he wants an authorization for the use of military force, then he should lead and tell us what he wants that authorization to be. And, frankly, for you to say that, well, we welcome it or whatever it is, of course, is an abrogation of the responsibilities of the President of the United States as Commander in Chief. So as we go through this charade, whether we have a vote or not in the next day or so before we go out is—almost makes it all irrelevant.

But I would hope in January working with the new chairman and the new ranking member and other members of this committee that the President of the United States would present an AUMF to the Congress and to this committee, and we could work together on it. But it has got to be led by the Commander in Chief, and, frankly, that is how the system works, and that is how it has worked every time.

Now, I would like to switch gears real quickly. Here is a Washington Post, "U.S. Backed Syrian Rebels Thwarted by Fighters Linked to al-Qaeda." "Time is Running Out For Obama in Syria." "Western Backed Syrian Rebels Are in Danger of Collapse Before Help Arrives." All of these facts are well-known to media experts, and the rebels are on the verge of collapse; they are getting beaten very badly. And one of the major reasons why they are getting beaten very badly is because they are subject to barrel bombing and air attacks from Bashar Assad.

So I guess my question to you again is what I asked you the time—and by the way, Ambassador James Jeffrey says times is not on our side—reconsider the no U.S. combat formations on the ground decision because you may have to either renege on that or you may have to fall off your very important mission of destroying ISIS. I think there is a gap between the two.

Ambassador Ford, ISIS is not something which drone strikes or F–16 strikes is going to contain because the Islamic State, let us face it, it is a state. So you do not destroy a state with drone strikes. You are going to require boots on the ground.

So what we are seeing, I would say to you, Mr. Secretary, is the incrementalism that I saw in the Vietnam war. We are seeing decisions made in a tight circle in the White House. We are seeing them incrementally implemented. We see, what, 200 troops, additional troops, then 500 more, and then 1,000 more.

Meanwhile, our Syrian rebels honestly do not understand why you will not protect them from Bashar's intense bombing campaign, and we are not attacking Bashar Assad. And we are asking these young people to fight and to die, and Bashar Assad, as you should know, is their major enemy, and we are not doing anything to stop Bashar Assad from barrel bombing them and slaughtering them.

Which—and this is the guy that has killed 200,000. This is the guy that has caused 3.5 million refugees. This is the guy that still has 150,000 people in his prisons in which he has treated with great atrocities.

Still one of the great mysteries to me in my life is these photos that were smuggled out by a guy named Caesar, got no response from the President of the United States or, frankly, from you. Should have been a casus belli.

So here we are with the rebels being routed because they are being attacked not only by Bashar Assad, but also extremist organizations called ISIS and others. And they are in the verge of collapse at least in one part of the country.

So now you are telling me we have a strategy to defeat Bashar Assad, and we have a strategy to defeat ISIS in Iraq and Syria, even though we are treating them as two separate battles, at least as far as strategy is concerned. Maybe you can respond to that and tell me what—how you justify morally telling young Syrians to go and fight in Syria and yet allow them to be barrel bombed by Bashar Assad, whose intensity of air strikes vastly increase those— are greater than those of U.S. air strikes on ISIS.

Secretary KERRY. Well, Senator, thank you.

Look, I think everybody is—there are certain frustrations here. We all understand that, and I will come back to Syria in one quick moment. But in point of fact, if I can correct you, you are not correct that when we have been here, there have not been instances where authorizations did not originate right here in the committee.

The year before I came here, on the Lebanon in 1983, it did. In 1991, when I was here, it originated here in the committee. George Herbert Walker Bush sent 350,000 troops to the Middle East to respond to the invasion of Kuwait.

Senator MCCAIN. Well, I will be glad to argue with you about it, but it is led—it has been led by the Presidents. I would appreciate if you would go on and——

Secretary KERRY. No, no.

Senator MCCAIN [continuing]. Justify how we can continue the massacre of brave young Syrians.

Secretary KERRY. I will come back to it, Senator. But I am going to answer the question.

Senator MCCAIN. I did not ask a question. I made a statement.

Secretary KERRY. And it was incorrect.

Senator MCCAIN. Now please move on——

Secretary KERRY. Well, your statement was incorrect, Senator.

Senator MCCAIN [continuing]. To the slaughter in Syria, please.

Secretary KERRY. Well, look, I am not going to sit here like a ping pong ball. I think that your statement was incorrect, and you know, everybody is accountable for what they say, and so are you. The fact is you are incorrect.

On January 8, 1991, Bush sent a letter here requesting it to adopt a resolution, and a few days later, Congress gave him what he asked for. And Congress originated it.

Senator MCCAIN. Yes, and he—and I was there, and he came over with a proposal. So go ahead.

Secretary KERRY. Did not come over——

Senator MCCAIN. He did come over with a proposal. You and I can argue about that if you want to. I was here, too. He came over with a proposal.

Secretary KERRY. He did not, and the record will show that.

Senator MCCAIN. The record will show that he did, if it was——

Secretary KERRY. And again, in Somalia in 1993, the committee likewise did it. And I served on the committee. I think I know what happened back then.

And Senator Biden, now Vice President, was on the committee, and we know what happened. So we can let the record speak to that.

With respect to what is happening, I think I was up front and stated that in the north they are seriously challenged. We understand that, and we have said that.

But the fact is that more is being done and more is being done than I can talk about here in this hearing, but the fact is that there are greater capacities being provided to the opposition. And our hope is that when we work things through with the Turks and over the next days, certain decisions will be made that, in fact, will provide greater capacity. But, yes, they are challenged today in the north.

But here is a reality. What we are doing to train them, the opposition, and what is being done with respect to ISIL, because the opposition, particularly in the north, has been fighting ISIL, and they have been fighting al-Nusra, and they have been fighting the regime.

What we are doing——

Senator MCCAIN. And we are allowing them to be barrel bombed.

Secretary KERRY. We are not allowing them to be barrel bombed.

Senator MCCAIN. We are not preventing them from being barrel bombed.

Secretary KERRY. Well, is the committee ready to vote?

How many votes are there in this committee for American forces to now go in——

Senator MCCAIN. That is not my answer. My answer is to give them the weapons they need, which they do not have.

Secretary KERRY. I just said to you that——

Senator MCCAIN. They do not have those weapons. It has been 3 years. It is 200,000 dead. I said——

Secretary KERRY. Senator, I just said to you there are things we cannot——

Senator MCCAIN. I said the last year when we were at—you were going to hit the trifecta. You hit it on Syria, you hit it on the Palestinians-Israelis, and now you are going to hit it on Iran. And now we are still not giving these people the support they need and deserve while 200,000 of them have been butchered.

Secretary KERRY. Senator, we are in the process right now, and I think you know this, there are certain things that are happening. And I do not think—I think it is a little disingenuous to suggest that nothing is being considered and nothing is happening when it is.

And the fact is that in a classified setting, you can go through precisely what is taking place, and I think you will have a better sense of what the options are.

Senator MCCAIN. I am sure there is young people that are dying in Syria are pleased to know that things are happening that we cannot even talk about. Disgraceful.

Secretary KERRY. Well, Senator, I mean, the rules of the Senate——

Senator MCCAIN. My time has expired.

Secretary KERRY. Now the rules of the Senate, you know, classified information is classified information. I mean, if you want to fight about that, you can. But——

Senator MCCAIN. I am not talking about classified information.

The CHAIRMAN. Time.

Senator MCCAIN. I want to know why we have not helped them for the last 3 or 4 years. They are fighting for freedom.

The CHAIRMAN. The time of the Senator has expired.

Secretary KERRY. Senator, we are helping them.

Senator MCCAIN. Appreciate it.

Secretary KERRY. We might not be helping them to your satisfaction, but there is a lot of help being given to them.

Senator MCCAIN. Not to their satisfaction.

The CHAIRMAN. Senator Murphy.

Senator MURPHY. Thank you very much, Mr. Chairman. Thank you and the ranking member and Secretary Kerry for taking this process so seriously.

I do not think this is a charade. I think whether or not we pass this through the House and through the Senate in the next few days, this has been a forcing mechanism. Without a submission from the administration, for whatever reason they may have, we needed this process. We needed these deliberations in order to get to a text that while it may not pass through both houses in the next few days, will be much more easily passed in January because of the work that this chairman and this committee has done and, hopefully, the discussions that Secretary Kerry is prepared to be a part of.

Two quick points, the second leading into a question. And I think what we are talking about here is a distinction between what the administration believes to be preferable, an authorization, and what many of us believe to be necessary, which is an authorization.

And just by way of explanation as to why many of us think that, I do think there is a difference in terms of what we believe ISIS to be. Many of us, respectfully, do not believe this is just a matter of a name change. This is an organization whose name is different, but who had a very specific tactical and strategical difference with al-Qaeda. There is a change in hierarchy.

And many of us worry that if a change in name and a change in tactic and a change in strategy and a change in hierarchy does not prompt us to pass a new authorization, we are not sure how we ever get out from underneath the original 2001 AUMF, which is why we think this is vitally necessary.

My second point is on this question of limitations. Senator Flake and Senator Johnson rattled off a list of authorizations that were fairly open-ended in nature, and that certainly has been the practice often of this Congress. But I can rattle you off a similar list of authorizations that the Congress has passed that have limitations.

You can start in the 1790s with our authorizations for action against the French navy. But fast forward to 1983, the authorization for military force in Lebanon, 1993 in Somalia, 2013 the authorization passed by this committee, all of them had different kinds of limitations. Limitations on time, limitations on tactics.

And so, it really is just a question of whether we think that the policy that we are talking about is so important that it should be in statutory language. And I think that is what you are hearing from many of us on this committee, that we understand that it is preferable to have a bipartisan bill, that in most circumstances, it is probably preferable to grant substantial deference to the administration.

But occasionally, there are questions that are so important that they are deserving of a statutory limitation, and that is why I think we are having to struggle over this question of ground forces because many of us believe that the deployment of ground forces in the Middle East today would essentially be fighting a fire with gasoline. That if we have learned anything from the last 10 years, it is that the massive deployment of American forces create twice as many foreign fighters and extremist fighters as they eliminate in the long run, and they provide a crutch for domestic governments to stand down and let us do all the work while they continue to stew in their dysfunction.

And I think part of our worry is that the reason why we do not have a Department of Defense witness here today is that there is substantial disagreement within the administration, that there is an element of the military which would like to have a serious conversation about the deployment of ground forces.

And we take—and I take at least—I will speak for myself. I take the I think you have termed it as a prohibition from the President incredibly seriously. I do not doubt for a second that you and the President are committed to keeping ground forces out of this equation. But many of us worry that that balance could tip or that the next administration could think differently.

And so, I guess my question would just be simple. It would be helpful to hear a little bit more about why you think, why the policy is such that you think it would be a bad idea, that it would be counter to our policy of degrading and defeating ISIL to insert ground forces into the equation? Because we sort of just take that for granted, but that clearly is a debate that is happening within foreign policy circles, within this committee, within the administration.

And I think it would be helpful just to hear how strongly that view is held within the Department of State and the Department of Defense and within the White House.

Secretary KERRY. Well, Senator, thank you for a very articulate statement of what the tensions are here, what is at stake, and I do not disagree with you. I think it is important for Congress to have that statutory statement of some kind or another.

And I assure you, President Obama, who served on this committee for, you know, 4 years and Senator Biden, then-Senator Biden, now Vice President, who served on this committee for about, what is it, you know, 30 years or near, both are huge supporters of the War Powers Act, as I am. He has lived by it, even in situations where he did not feel like he had to necessarily strictly send up, he sent it up. He always moved on the side of caution and of compliance.

And they believe it is important to have an appropriate authorization of military force. But as President of the United States, he also believes that his constitutional authority is vital and his ability as Commander in Chief to fully empower his military to be able to effect what he needs should not be micromanaged and restrained in a way that might eliminate, might eliminate some option they may need at some point in time.

It would be hard to imagine, given the experience of Iraq and all that we learned about our forces on the ground and these reactions of people indigenously that you talk about, that, you know, that someone is going to voluntarily say we ought to have major ground force for a long period of time.

I mean, what we are really talking about is protecting against exigencies, emergencies, certain circumstances that may or may not arise. For instance, like the rescue effort, tragically that did not work, of Luke Somers the other day. Would that have been envisioned within it? I do not know. I do not think so. But there are other circumstances that may arise, and we cannot predict them all. Nobody can.

So all we are trying to do is preserve, and I think, as again I say the duration, the timeframe here is such. And I think you, yourselves, you have to trust your own power in the Congress and the ability of Congress, if there were suddenly movements to do this, I cannot imagine it being funded. I cannot imagine that, you know, there is not going to be a hue and cry that would be overwhelming in reaction to that, absent some, again, extraordinary circumstances that merited that kind of response.

But do you want to pre-guess that? Do you want to predetermine what you—then you are tangled up in a statutory knot and trying to get out of it. I think the better part of wisdom here is to try to maintain an adequate level of flexibility, but at the same time preserve your prerogative through the duration of time, et cetera.

Now the administration has said the President is prepared to have his people sit carefully, work through this language, try to see how to balance these equities. You know, what he wants is the broadest vote possible. Get everybody in a place where they are comfortable, if that is achievable, and I think it ought to be.

Senator MURPHY. I appreciate that. I think the more that you review the chairman's draft, you will see that that specific hypothetical that you posed is covered by one of these exceptions. And I would imagine almost every other hypothetical that could be presented is going to be covered by the exceptions in the draft.

But I look forward to that process. I do not think there is reason to be as scared of these limitations as you may be, given what has already been drafted.

Secretary KERRY. Well, if they are all covered, maybe it is better to say something about no enduring activity or no enduring ground—I mean, there is a way to cover it maybe with one sentence. Let us think about other ways of doing.

All I am saying is, folks, let us agree to try to find a way to talk this through without posturing.

The CHAIRMAN. As I turn to—as I turn to Senator Barrasso, let me just say on that particular issue, page 5 of the draft AUMF says that troops are permitted for the protection or rescue of members of the U.S. Armed Forces or United States citizens from imminent danger posed by ISIS. So it envisioned that——

Secretary KERRY. But I have other examples——

The CHAIRMAN. I am sure we could throw out 100 and I am not sure that there would be language that could cover all 100 of them. But we were certainly—as I say, I am happy to see the language, if that can be envisioned.

Senator Barrasso.

Senator BARRASSO. Thank you, Mr. Chairman.

Thank you, Mr. Secretary.

Today's hearing on the authorization of the use of military force against ISIL, I believe, is critically important. Declaring war or authorizing the use of military force is one of the most serious responsibilities of Congress. There can hardly be a task more weighty and solemn than sending our Nation's sons or daughters into harm's way to protect our interests.

So I believe President Obama has an obligation to Congress and to the American people to spell out the direct threat posed by ISIL, to outline his strategy for comprehensively destroying ISIL, and request the authorities he needs to successfully complete the mission. I believe ISIL is a threat to our homeland, and I support efforts to eliminate this terrorist threat.

Our committee is debating the authorization for the use of military force while the President has already been taking offensive military actions against ISIL for months. President Obama has not submitted a request outlining that authorization that he is seeking from Congress.

Normally, when the executive branch wants an authorization for the use of military force, it formally requests that legislative authorization and then is actively involved in negotiating over the language and advocating its passage. That is how the 2001 AUMF was developed. But we see no similar effort on behalf of the Obama administration.

So in the absence of the administration's specific request or submission of a proposal for authorization, some Members of Congress are more interested in placing limitations in the AUMF and tying the hands of the President and our Nation's generals. Whether it is geographical or operational limitations, I think these limitations are misguided and dangerous.

Congress should either be authorizing the use of force or not authorizing force. Congress should not try to micromanage a war through an authorization.

So if the administration had provided military and intelligence witnesses, and the chairman has already made a comment about your willingness to come forward, but not having all of the abilities to answer all of the questions. You know, I would have asked how the limitation of the use of ground troops would impact the military's planning and the ability to respond to conditions on the ground.

So since they are not here, I ask you how do we ensure that any AUMF continues to allow the United States to strike and destroy ISIS should it expand outside of any limitations which may be included in an AUMF that is being offered?

Secretary KERRY. Well, that is precisely why we are trying to work out this question of the limitations. Because I cannot answer it otherwise.

Senator BARRASSO. So you believe that there should not be limitations?

Secretary KERRY. I said we are prepared to embrace a clarification, a process by which there is an understanding of how we can balance these equities. It may require some kind of restraint that we feel would not abrogate the Commander in Chief responsibilities. I think there is a way to work at it, and that is what we are offering to try to do.

But you know, or example, what about non-U.S. hostage or prisoner? I mean, that might be a situation. You can run through all kinds of things here. The point is we are just trying to preclude sending restraint messages to folks that we are trying to defeat and degrade and at the same time balance the equities of the concerns people have about the open-endedness that we have lived with in the past. And it is a legitimate concern.

I think everybody ought to try to help find the way to work that through, and in the doing so, we can ensure that we have the kind of broad-based bipartisan resolution that we deserve.

Senator BARRASSO. Do you think there are additional specific authorities that the administration needs that they currently do not have to degrade and destroy ISIL?

Secretary KERRY. At this point in time? You mean the authorization we are giving at this point?

Senator BARRASSO. Yes.

Secretary KERRY. No. I think the President feels that he has the full authority, both constitutionally and through the current AUMF. But we acknowledge that it needs refining. We acknowledge that there is a gap in time and a sufficient differential in what we are fighting that the American people are owed a more precise articulation that meets the current moment, and that is what the President is saying we should have.

Senator BARRASSO. Mr. Secretary, your predecessor, Hillary Clinton, recently stated in a speech at Georgetown University that America needs to show respect for our enemies and empathize with their perspective and point of view.

ISIS terrorists are not going to simply go away. We cannot ignore them and hope that they will embrace our values. And we certainly cannot empathize and show respect to people who have brutally murdered brave Americans.

So do you believe, as Secretary of State, that a key solution to our enemies such as ISIS and al-Qaeda is ''showing respect'' and ''empathizing with their perspective and point of view''?

Secretary KERRY. Well, you know, I missed the first part of the quote. I apologize. What was it? Empathize?

Senator BARRASSO. Hillary at Georgetown recently said that America needs to show respect for our enemies and empathize with their perspective and point of view.

Secretary KERRY. Yes, well, I do not think she was referring— I am confident. I know she was not referring to a group like Daesh. I think she is—you know, I think in terms of what she meant, there is no question in my mind, she is referring to those out there with whom we are not actively fighting or engaged in war but who are behaving in ways that are clearly opposed to our interests.

And there are plenty of people in that status, regrettably, whether it is in the Middle East in certain countries or in other parts of the world. I mean, we have a lot of tensions right now with Russia, and it is clear that any analysis of what is happening in Ukraine and how you deal with it or in other parts of the world requires you to look very carefully at all their posturing and where it comes from and what may be involved and how one might be able to defuse it.

So I have no doubt that does not include a group like Daesh, and I think it would be unfair to insinuate that it does.

Senator BARRASSO. Thank you, Mr. Chairman.

The CHAIRMAN. Thank you.

Before I turn to Senator Kaine, you know, a lot has been made here about placing restrictions on AUMFs and the suggestion that there is no precedent for Congress doing that. That is simply not true.

The fact is, is that most AUMFs historically have limited the type of forces deployed into harm's way, the geographic scope, and the period of time. It is declarations of war, which is not what we are doing, nor what the administration has asked us for, that have typically authorized the President to use all military means available to the United States for unlimited duration.

My text is clearly not a declaration of war, nor has the administration asked us for a declaration of war, and several of my colleagues have noted this. But you know, some of the AUMFs that have included restrictions are the 1993 Somalia AUMF, which authorized United States Armed Forces in a limited way to protect United States personnel and assist in the short-term security of U.N. units; the 1983 Lebanon AUMF that prohibited offensive actions.

The 2013 Syria AUMF that passed through this committee, I think one of its high-water marks, in a bipartisan way expressly did not authorize the use of the United States Armed Forces on the ground in Syria for the purpose of combat operations.

We have a span of nearly 30 years, to take recent history, in which AUMFs have had limitations. So the suggestion that having limitations is a historical aberration, that is just simply not the case.

Senator Kaine, who has been greatly involved in this issue, and along with Senator Paul, their amendments have driven us to this—to this moment.

So, Senator Kaine.

Senator KAINE. Thank you, Mr. Chairman.

And thank you, Secretary Kerry. You have not been before us to receive the thanks of this committee for some of your diplomacy, the diplomatic efforts to help reform the Government in Iraq, the diplomatic efforts to break the electoral impasse in Afghanistan. I want to thank you for those because those efforts were important.

I want to thank you for your efforts on behalf of the administration to build the coalition that is fighting against ISIL. Senator King and I went to Al Udeid Air Base in Qatar in early October and went to the CAOC, Combined Air Operations Center, and we witnessed the coalition in action. Full-screen videos, data coming in, United States, Saudi, UAE, Dutch, Belgian, French, Canadian, United Kingdom, Qataris trading information, making decisions together in both the Syrian and Iraqi theaters. Very, very impressive.

You deserve our thanks for that. But we cannot do military action without Congress, and we are currently in what the administration has described, beginning in late August, as a war against ISIL. Those were the phase that both Secretary Hagel has used, the President has used it. Since we moved from the immediate protection of U.S. Embassy personnel in Baghdad and Erbil, an effort to take back a dam in the middle of August, the President said we have gone on offense against ISIL.

Yesterday, we passed 4 months. We are in month 5 of an air strike campaign that has involved 1,100 plus air strikes, as you testified; 1,500 combat train and assist advisers on the ground in the theater, another 1,500 authorized to go. The cost of this to the American taxpayer has now been in excess of $1 billion.

And three American troops have been killed supporting Operation Inherent Resolve, and I just think we ought to at least mention their names. October 1, Marine Corporal Jordan Spears from Memphis, Indiana. October 23, Marine Lance Corporal Sean Neal from Riverside, California. December 1, Captain William H. Dubois of New Castle, Colorado, an Air Force captain.

We are at war, and Congress has not yet really done a darned thing about it.

I respect the comments that the ranking member, Senator Corker, who I deeply respect, said earlier about the process of this is not ideal. It was not ideal when Senator Paul and I tried to file an AUMF as an amendment to an international water bill last week, but if we had not done it, we would not even been doing this at all until January.

Congress has been silent about this. I do not think we weaken our Nation so much with an unwieldy process as we weaken our Nation when we do not take seriously the most somber responsibility that Congress has, which is to engage around the declaration at the beginning, not 5 months in, at the beginning about whether we should initiate war.

Constitutionally, it is required. I am driven by a more important value. I do not think it is fair to ask people, like these three, to risk their lives, to give their lives in a mission if Congress has not had a debate and put their thumbprint on it and said this is in the national interest. If we are not willing to do that, how can we ask people to risk their lives?

I think it would be foolish to leave here this week or next, to adjourn, wait until January when we come back. January 8, the first week we are back, we would now be into the 6th month of war without Congress taking any action.

This is not about a quest to just seem relevant. For those of us who do not believe that the 2001 or 2002 authorizations give this a legal authority, every day we have been on offense without Congress we believe is an unauthorized war. We believe it is a congressional abdication of our oath of office and of our fundamental constitutional responsibilities.

There is a difference of opinion between the executive and the legislature on this. But remember, this is about an argument about what power the legislature gave to the Executive in 2001 and 2002, and you might not be surprised to know that those of us in the legislative branch have a pretty strong opinion about what that power was and what it was not.

I do not think we can wait until January or February. So we should act. The administration has not done your own draft? Hey, we have got a deadline tomorrow to file amendments to this one. First degree amendments at 9 a.m. Second degree amendments at 6 a.m.

You say we are close. Offer your own wordsmith and I am sure the chairman will make sure that when we talk about it, we can consider the administration's position. But we cannot afford to wait and get into the 6th month of a war without Congress saying a mumbling word about this.

I think I know the answer to this, but I do want to put it on the record, and I want to ask you a question. I want to ask you a question about whether the President or the administration's position have changed from what the President has said. And I am going to read you five statements.

August 9, 2014. ''Number one, I have been very clear that we are not going to have United States combat troops in Iraq again.''

September 10, 2014. ''As I have said before, these American forces will not have a combat mission. We will not get dragged into another ground war in Iraq.''

On that same date, ''It will not involve American combat troops fighting on foreign soil.''

September 17, 2014. ''The American forces that have been deployed to Iraq do not and will not have a combat mission. They will support Iraqi forces on the ground as they fight for their country against these terrorists. I will not commit you and the rest of our armed forces to be fighting another ground war in Iraq.''

And finally, on September 18, 2014. ''I will not commit our troops to fighting another ground war in Iraq or in Syria.''

Has the President's position or has the administration's position, as evidenced by these clear and unequivocal statements, changed?

Secretary KERRY. No.

Senator KAINE. Let me address the constitutional question that the chairman brought up a minute ago because I do think it is important. Is there precedent for restrictions or limitations in authorization? Senator Murphy dealt with this as well.

I would recommend to all my colleagues an article, "Congressional Authorization and the War on Terrorism," authored by Jack Goldsmith and Curtis Bradley, May of 2005 in the Harvard Law Review. It is an extensive review of the constitutional power of Congress with respect to military authorizations.

And it begins with a case that went to the Supreme Court dealing with the quasi wars that Senator Murphy mentioned against the French naval authorities in the 1790s. Congress granted limited authorizations.

The authorizations "did not authorize the President to use all of the armed forces of the United States or to conduct military incursions beyond specified military targets, and they limited the geographical scope of the authorized conflict to the high seas." Navy only. No ground troops.

Most authorizations to use force in U.S. history have been of this limited or partial nature. The constitutional argument on this is clear. The President's intent, as stated repeatedly to the American public and the military, is clear. There has been no change in that position, according to your testimony today.

The language in the chairman's mark is not a restriction at all. It is attempting to carry out exactly how the President has described the mission. And as far as exigencies and contingencies go, I give a lot of praise to the chairman for trying to listen to all of us, listen to the administration through those seven conversations, and put a mark together that—that covers the contingencies or exigencies that we can think of.

And finally, the President always has the power under Article II to use any forces, including ground forces, to repel an imminent threat to the United States by ISIL or by any other group or nation. That power is absolute. No one on this committee questions it. But in terms of putting restrictions into this, it has been done since the 1790s without any constitutional suggestion.

I would hope you might offer some thoughts tomorrow as we are contemplating amendments so that Thursday we can do this. But I do not think we can wait until the 6th month of this war without Congress to finally begin to express the will of the Article I branch.

Thank you, Mr. Chair.

The CHAIRMAN. Senator Paul.

Secretary KERRY. Can I just make a comment quickly?

The CHAIRMAN. Quickly.

Secretary KERRY. I will not take long, Senator Paul.

Just very quickly, first of all, that is a very articulate summary and argument with respect to your particular position on it. I think historically in most AUMFs and most debates about whether we should be using force or not, depending on who is President and depending on the balance in the Senate and the House and so forth, there tends to be an argument de novo, so to speak. And people come in and say, hey, Presidential power and the Article II and know there have been restraints. And that is going to apply to every situation, as it does here, as we are now debating.

The question is, is there an effective way to achieve this goal that, given the balance of interests, et cetera, in this situation at this moment, given this particular fight, could achieve the goal? Differently perhaps from the way it has been laid out, but without losing the impact or the effect.

I think there may be some ways, and I suggested a couple. One is through the duration. Another may be through some kind of language that talks about no enduring combat operation or whatever, but that is different and that avoids having to get into this specific discussion of all the kind of instances, which you are trying to cover, Mr. Chairman, respectfully, in this.

So I would just say to you, with all genuine effort to try to achieve this goal of getting a maximum vote, I would just suggest that maybe a better way than kind of just doing it by amendment is to pre-work the amendment or to find out if you could come together and get an agreement so that you are doing it either by consensus or agreement on that amendment rather than just fighting out the amendments, and you have a vote, and it is up or down. And you still do not resolve the fundamental problem.

So all the administration is saying to you is we want an AUMF. Yet whatever has happened to date—I am not going to go backward—we would like to work it through in a way with you that comes out with the strongest possible result. Because the goal here is to get a result that has an impact for our allies, for our troops on the field who are deployed, and particularly for the coalition and for ISIL itself to understand our intent.

And I do not want to see that diminished by whatever amendment process may flow without the adequate input.

The CHAIRMAN. Senator Paul.

Senator PAUL. Thank you, and thank you for your testimony.

I think there is no greater responsibility for any legislator than the debate over when we send our brave young men and women to war. The Constitution is quite clear that this responsibility lies with Congress.

Madison wrote in The Federalist Papers when describing the congressional authority requirement, he wrote that the executive branch is the branch most prone to war, and therefore, we have with studied care vested that power in the legislature.

I think for 5 months, we have been derelict in our duty. I think we have had great leaders in our past. When FDR came the day after Pearl Harbor, he came before a joint session of Congress to ask for war. George W. Bush came within 2 weeks after 9/11 to a joint session of Congress with the same request.

I think this President has been derelict. But I think at the same time, there is enough blame to go around for Congress, who has also been derelict in their duty. There has been some gnashing of teeth that some Senators had the temerity to offer this as an amendment to the water bill. Had we not offered this as an amendment to the water bill, there would be no debate over war at this point.

So I accept that blame as a badge of honor and pledge to continue in the new Congress and to amend any bill that comes before the Foreign Relations Committee with the use of authorization of force until we do finally have a debate and a vote before the full Congress, as we should.

There was some discussion, and you have said the administration is opposed to a geographic limit. Some on our side are basically for no limits at all. But after watching what has happened in the last 15 years and watching the gymnastics, the mental gymnastics that tries to use an authorization of force that was intended to be used against those who attacked us on 9/11, to say ISIS has anything to do with them I think is an absurd notion and an argument for why we need to be very careful what authorization we give and very strict in what authority we give to the President.

For example, the administration, through your testimony, says they believe no geographic limit. Senator Udall brought forward a great example. He said you know what? There are groups in Libya, Algeria, Yemen, and Saudi Arabia who have pledged allegiance to the Islamic State, and I am going to give you a chance to revise your answer because you very quickly said, of course, that is why we need no geographic limit.

Okay. Tomorrow, Medina. Medina, Saudi Arabia, pledges their allegiance to ISIS. This resolution will authorize you to bomb Medina, Saudi Arabia. Is that the message you want to send to the world that you want the authority, the unlimited authority to attack geographically anywhere in the world if someone pledges their allegiance to the Islamic State?

That is absolutely why I cannot vote for any resolution that does not have a geographic restraint, and realize the message we send, if that is the message we are sending, that if Medina or Mecca pledges allegiance to the Islamic State, they are open to being bombed by the United States. That is a very, very scary and I think a wrong-headed message to be sending to the Middle East.

Your comments, please?

Secretary KERRY. Well, my comment is, Senator, I think there is a responsibility to pick logical and legitimate kinds of options, number one. And number two, to make a presumption in the sanity of the President of the United States, nobody is talking about bombing everywhere.

Senator PAUL. Let us be very explicit and limit it then.

Secretary KERRY. No. Senator, that is precisely what the Constitution—you are a student of the Constitution, and you pride yourself in upholding it and being a strict constructionist. And being a strict constructionist, I do not think you should put those limitations on the power of the Executive.

If you want to get into it as a declaration of war, you certainly have the right to try to do that. But I would counsel you also that no declaration of war has taken place since World War II. Since World War II.

And no President has come here, including George Bush, who you cited erroneously as having done so. He did not come and ask for a declaration of war. He asked for an authorization for the use of force.

Senator PAUL. I did not say he came for a declaration of war, but he did come as a leader before the joint session of Congress.

Secretary KERRY. But let me just finish. Let me be crystal clear here. You know, if you are going to be strictly constructionist and adhere to the Constitution in terms of what you are arguing about the right, declaration of war, it would be a mistake to ask for a declaration of war. You want a, you know, use of military force because a declaration of war has only been used against states.

Senator PAUL. I am really not making that argument. I am making the argument currently for a limit of geographic nature to whether it is a use of force or a declaration of war, that it should be limited because here is the problem. You are sending a message to the Middle East that no city is off limits, that if any city in the Middle East declares an allegiance to the Islamic State that you would be justified and you would have the authority to bomb them.

Secretary KERRY. Senator, that statement is being made without any input or, frankly, consideration for the limits and strictures within which the United States of America is currently operating. We have some of the most extraordinary self-imposed restraints on our checklists for where and when and how we might use force even where we have been authorized to use force.

And you need to review that. You need to go find out what restraints our military is currently operating under.

Senator PAUL. There is a very important restraint, and that is the Constitution that says Congress initiates war. You went to war in Libya without congressional authority. You have now been at war for 5 months without constitutional or congressional authority.

Secretary KERRY. We did not go to war in Libya. It depends how you look at these. I mean, this term of "war" is, frankly, I think——

Senator PAUL. Oh, I forgot. That was kinetic action?

Secretary KERRY. I think that we are not going to war in the way that we went to war in Iraq. We are not going to war in the way that we went to war in Afghanistan.

We are engaged in what people want to call a war and can call a war certainly, and we have. But it is very restrained and different in scope.

Senator PAUL. But that is why we should be very explicit.

Secretary KERRY. Which is why—which is—let me just finish. Which is why we are in favor of an authorization for use of military force which defines what it is.

Senator PAUL. Right.

Secretary KERRY. But this is different. I mean, you need to look at the checklist our people go through with respect to whether or not they might take a shot at somebody. You need to look at the restraints the President of the United States has put on our military—let me finish.

Senator PAUL. This is not about whether you are restraining. It is about the division of power and the balance of power between the branches of Government.

Secretary KERRY. No, it is bigger than that. It is really bigger than that. It is not just about the division of power. It is about what you are trying to achieve and how you can achieve it. And also about how you use power.

But if you do not look at what you are trying to achieve and what the methodologies are, the tools that you have at your disposal, you are not going to get very far.

Senator PAUL. Let me ask one quick question to finish, and that was last year when you came before the committee for the Syrian AUMF, you said that there is no problem in our having a language that has zero capacity for American troops on the ground within the authorization the President is asking for.

This was against a regime that some would argue is more formidable than ISIS, has greater assets for fighting war, and would be a much more significant opponent, or at least equally as significant as ISIS, but many would argue much greater. And there, you were willing to accept that you would have a prohibition on ground forces, but today you are unwilling to accept a prohibition on ground forces.

How would you compare the relative strength of the two opponents, and why would you accept no ground forces against the Syrian regime that has an air force and has many more weapons at its command and a larger army than ISIS?

Secretary KERRY. Are you going to let me answer this in full?

Senator PAUL. Absolutely.

Secretary KERRY. Because I want to answer it. Very specifically, because it is an entirely different situation, what we were asking for in the case of the limited authority to have a limited strike against Assad at that time was entirely focused on degrading his capacity to deliver chemical weapons and sending a limited message. And we came here with great specificity about the serious limitations on what we were seeking.

So asking for—allowing that restraint at that time had no imposition on the capacity to carry out the mission. The mission was going to be without troops, without ground forces. It was designed that way. It would have been executed that way, and we were losing absolutely nothing whatsoever in the potential because we had no intention of putting forces in to do what we were going to do and achieve what we were going to achieve.

Now we achieved——

Senator PAUL. But that sounds similar to your statements that you have made about this war.

Secretary KERRY. No. Because the President acknowledges, as any President would, as all of our military would, ask any of the people who are being asked to implement this strategy whether they feel comfortable knowing that they have been limited and what option might or might not be available to them if they have to do it.

Now the President has made it clear it is not his policy. And I have never seen anybody more adamant about that and more clear in every statement he has made. They were all quoted by Senator Kaine. Five times or four times in the month of September, he has reiterated it.

But that does not mean that you want to take away what might be conceivably necessary at some point in time in certain circumstances. The President is absolutely clear about his policy.

But I have to say to you that by virtue of the President's decision to use force, and thank you to this committee for voting and having made clear Congress was moving in that direction, guess what? Instead of 1 or 2 days of bombing in order to send a message that you should not use these, we have got to deal with Russia to get 100 percent of the weapons out.

And that is because you did not limit it. You left it open, and there was a question that we might, in fact, do what we said we were going to do.

That was—actually, that is another moment where for the first time in history during a conflict, we have removed all the known declared chemical weapons from a country. And believe me, thank God we did. Because today ISIL is in there controlling half the country, and imagine what would happen if they would gain control of those chemical weapons.

So it is a completely different situation, Senator, where you have, you know, a very limited goal, limited stated, and you are willing to live under it. And the Executive says I will live under it.

Here, you have an Executive who does not have as limited a goal, but who has said already he is going to limit his means of achieving the goal but does not want to be hamstrung in every other way with respect to the constitutional authorities that I know——

Senator PAUL. But for those of us who believe——

The CHAIRMAN. The Senator's time——

Senator PAUL [continuing]. Another Iraq war, that is why we are concerned about limiting this.

Secretary KERRY. I well understand that.

The CHAIRMAN. I know both of you would like to engage in a debate, but I have to get to another member.

Just for the record, the Syria AUMF did, obviously had a limitation on ground forces, did not have a limitation as to the other wherewithal that the administration wanted to prevent chemical weapons.

Senator Markey.

Senator MARKEY. Thank you, Mr. Chairman.

And thank you, Mr. Secretary, for your excellent work on behalf of our country. We thank you for your incredible service over these last 2 years.

I am one of the few members of Congress who voted for the authorization of military force in 2001 and who voted for the authorization of military force in 2002. When I look back at that, I never contemplated that it would authorize 2.5 million American military personnel to go to Iraq and Afghanistan. I never would have envisioned that 670,000 of them would now be declared officially disabled, that 270,000 of them would be treated for post traumatic stress syndrome, that the health care bills would now have risen to over $1 trillion, separate from the $1 trillion spent on those conflicts.

So it is a very timely debate that we are having for all of us, huh? We need to just turn the page and move on to this next stage because the use of those old authorizations do a disservice to this institution and to this country.

So from my perspective, obviously, we are trying our best as a Congress to ensure that we do not invoke the law of unintended consequences, as we did with those first two authorizations of military force. I never imagined that George Bush would interpret the

2002 authorization the way he did, but he did. And even as we debate this authorization, it will go into the next Presidency.

And so, we have to be careful necessarily. And so, I think that is why we are all being very cautious here because we have lived through this recent American history, and we do not want to repeat it.

So from my perspective, Mr. Secretary, I am looking at Iraq right now, looking for some hope. You have had some breakthroughs. They have named a Sunni Defense Minister, and there seems to be some progress that would obviate the need for American combat troops on the ground in Iraq.

Could you talk a little bit about that and the hopes that you have that the Iraqi Sunnis would start fighting ISIS and stop fighting the Iraqi Security Forces? Could you just talk a little bit about that and how hopeful you are that we are on the correct path in that country to reseal the Syrian-Iraqi border?

Secretary KERRY. Well, thank you. Thank you, Senator, and thank you for your generous comments. And I appreciate your comment very much about your vote and what you did or did not contemplate, and I certainly would agree with you, having been here then and voting in that period of time.

Which is why President Obama and Vice President Biden really are both so committed to an AUMF that appropriately reflects where we are today. And I know he believes very deeply that we will be stronger as a country if we have this broad vote that I have talked about.

So I would say to all of you, notwithstanding the passion with which you approach this sense of the mistakes that may have been made and the open-endedness of war, et cetera, I do believe there are ways to craft this so that it is not open-ended and so that there are the sufficient levels of clarifications about administration, et cetera, without getting into something that is going to be impossible to get that broad vote from. And I ask you to keep that in mind.

What we get for a vote here is a very important part of what we are trying to achieve. The unanimity, the breadth and scope of support is a message to everybody involved in this—the coalition, our troops, you know, our closest allies, and even to the people we are fighting.

So I appreciate your focusing on Iraq because, in fact, we were deeply involved from the moment the President made the comment that we have to know we had a government we could work with in order to be able to commit to doing something. Because anything we tried to do in Iraq if we had not had a governmental transformation would never have worked, and we would be in a really difficult situation here.

Who knows whether ISIL would have been in Baghdad or whether Iran might have decided to go even further in to be involved, et cetera. There are whole bunch of major strategic permutations that could have unfolded, but we became deeply engaged diplomatically, and a superb team worked hard, working with our allies in the region to help the Iraqis be able to make the choices they made. And they made them.

It was difficult. They got a new speaker. The current speaker gave up his position and moved out. That took a lot of effort, and that opened up the door to the selection of a Kurd President. And that opened up the door to the selection of a new Prime Minister.

And when Ayatollah Sistani and others weighed in, there were a whole series of events that took place that brought about this change in government. And just last week, we were in Brussels with the new Prime Minister, Prime Minister Abadi, speaking to some 60 entities and countries about his efforts to bring people together, to recognize there was no room for the kind of sectarian divide that had torn the place apart previously.

Now Iran plays a hand here. It has got to be stated. There is an impact in Iraq with Iran because Iraq is 80 percent Shia, and there are interests. And historically—and other interests, I might add, religious sites, other kinds of things.

So, hopefully, the Shia militia, with whom the current administration is currently working to try to restrain them from violence against Sunni, and the Sunni tribal chiefs can come together with confidence that the military is evolving in a way that together with their concept of a national guard and with new respect within the government itself for an inclusivity and participation, that can unite people around the goal of focusing only on getting rid of Daesh.

Our feeling is that the training is coming along, that with the oil deal and other measures being taken, there is a constant effort being made to try to unite the government. There are still tensions.

Importantly, regional efforts are taking place. When we had the meeting in Jeddah, which was the beginning of the organization of the coalition within the region, the Foreign Minister of Saudi Arabia, Saud al-Faisal, promptly stated, ''We will recognize the new government. We will open up diplomatic relations, and we will exchange visits.'' That is happening.

Prime Minister Davutoglu of Turkey visited Iraq. The Emirati Foreign Minister, Abdullah bin Zayed, visited Iraq. So there is a regional shift taking place.

Now we obviously hope it holds. We will work diligently with them. But this combination of training with the military, desectarianizing—I mean undoing the sectarian divide that has taken place, building confidence among the Sunni is going to be a long process, but it has started. And it is having some impact, and it has the potential of having a profound impact on Iraq itself.

Senator MARKEY. And may I just say, John, that that is what the American people want. They want a diplomatic resolution of this issue amongst the people who live in both Iraq and in Syria and the surrounding countries. That is what they want more than anything, and they do not want another open-ended opportunity for a commitment of another 2.5 million Americans into that region.

Because the potential is there for that, and there are some members on this committee, in fact, who believe that it should be open-ended. And I just think that that debate is the debate that we have to have this time before we go more deeply.

Secretary KERRY. I appreciate it, Senator.

The CHAIRMAN. Senator——

Senator MARKEY. And I thank you for your great service.

Secretary KERRY. Can I just say that President Obama deserves credit, Mr. Chairman——

The CHAIRMAN. Mr. Secretary, we are going to have to synthesize this because we have been here 31/2 hours, and I still want to get to Senator Durbin.

Secretary KERRY. Fifteen seconds.

The CHAIRMAN. Yes, go ahead.

Secretary KERRY. President Obama deserves credit for having made the decision, which I think was key, that he was not going to move until they began to make the moves to put a government change in place. And that is really what leveraged this entire effort, and I think he deserves credit for having done that.

The CHAIRMAN. Senator Durbin will have the last word here in questions.

Senator DURBIN. My apologies, Mr. Secretary. We have a hearing on the state of civil rights in America that was scheduled that coincided with this, and I presided and could not attend this. But I have had a pretty good summary of what happened from my staff.

Secretary and Senator, you can recall the debates in 2001 and 2002, and some of us who voted against the invasion of Iraq but felt that we did the right thing in voting to go after al-Qaeda, I do not think anybody envisioned we were voting for the longest war in the history of the United States of America and that our pursuit of al-Qaeda would take us into this situation today.

And apparently, some within the administration believe that my vote then was an approval for what we are doing today. Whether I agree or disagree with the President's actions today, I think that is a stretch to call this an al-Qaeda operation, even after al-Qaeda has disavowed Daesh or ISIS, whatever the current nomenclature is.

Mr. Secretary, what it gets down to is this. The President has said there will be no ground troops. When General Dempsey came and testified before Congress and said there may be ground troops, the administration was quick to correct him and say we have no plans for ground troops.

Many of us believe that we ought to stand by the President's public statement about no ground troops when it comes to the authorization of use for military force. Our fear is that if we do not, either this President or some future President will drag us into another deep, long-lasting, bloody, almost pointless conflict.

I am troubled that that is the new position of the administration to want authority for ground troops. I thought that issue was clear.

Secretary KERRY. It is. It is absolutely clear. There is nothing that has changed. The President does not intend to, not planning to. There is no thought in his head of using ground troops.

Senator DURBIN. Why then object to our saying that clearly in the authorization for use of military force?

Secretary KERRY. Because what is contemplated by that, I think, Senator, is clearly this notion that we are not going to do some big deployment and get involved in an enormous war. But if there is some one-time operation that requires X, Y, or Z. Now you have tried to cover some of them. You have tried to make that clear.

You are already accepting that. But the issue is can you provide an adequate guarantee of an exception for everything that may or may not arise in that context only? There is no effort here to slide or try to change this. There is not going to be a big—there is no effort to do that.

But all we are suggesting is we think there is a capacity to clarify, to try to work this through in a way that could bring both sides of this dais together in an effort to have a more powerful message in this vote and a clearer AUMF. And I think we can achieve that.

Senator DURBIN. I will just say the chairman and ranking member have been so patient, and I am not going to ask any further questions other than to say, Mr. Secretary, this is important, critically important. It is not just important in terms of those whose lives will be at risk and what we are trying to achieve in the Middle East. But it has an importance that relates to our constitutional responsibilities, each of us.

Secretary KERRY. Absolutely.

Senator DURBIN. And I think that if we do not assert ourselves and our constitutional responsibility when it comes to this conflict, we are remiss. I do not want to be condemned by future generations for walking away from this responsibility. If we can work out an agreement, fine. If we cannot, we still have a responsibility to pass this authorization. I hope we do it before we leave.

Secretary KERRY. We have three former members of this committee who are asking for the authorization who agree with you but would like to see us do it in a way that gets the vote we talked about.

Senator DURBIN. Thanks, Mr. Chairman.

The CHAIRMAN. Senator Corker, final remarks?

Senator CORKER. I want to thank you for having the hearing. I think this is much better than what was contemplated last week.

I want to thank the Secretary for coming in today and providing some principles that I really believe we can all build on.

And I do applaud the President and you for making sure that in Iraq we had a different government situation there before we committed. I think that was a good thing.

I do want to say again I think that we can get to a place where there is that broader support. I really believe that. I am going to say something that my friends on this side of the aisle will disagree with. The reason we are here is a total failure of the President to lead on this issue and to send something up here.

And so, we find ourselves divided when, in essence, we all want the same thing. We want to authorize the President to be able to do the things that are necessary to deal with ISIS. I mean, I think we are united there. And the reason we are in this cluster, which is where we are, is because the President has not really sought that authorization.

Now today you came closer, not quite all the way there. But you came closer to asking for an explicit authorization. Came closer. A better approach to me would be for you to send up the language that I think people have asked for, and there might be some common ground here, more than we think.

But the one piece that I think is missing by not asking explicitly is we do not have the opportunity to really delve into the strategy of this, and that, you know, we are talking about limitations in writing. But one of the things that we have not had the opportunity to do, and I think anyone who attended the classified briefing we had a month ago with military leadership and others, I do not think anybody left there believing that we understood how we were going to deal with ISIS. I mean, I think there were a lot of gaps that we did not understand.

So what is missing is not just the document, but it is also what is missing is when you seek something explicitly, we have the opportunity to probe how you are going to go about doing that. Now we just heard from leaders in the region, several of us with a meeting. I know there is tremendous division over the Assad issue. Assad is the magnet for ISIS in the first place.

So I do hope that we will continue. I hope that you will send up explicit language. I hope that we will have the opportunity to understand how we are going to go forward.

One of the reasons we ended up in a 12- or 13-year war is there was not any of this discussion on the front end. It did not happen. But it is not just the language. It is actually understanding how we are going to go about dealing with this, and that is a massive missing element here.

So I want to thank the Secretary for being here. I think he has conducted himself fairly well, except for evading the issue of the explicit request. I thank him for the principles.

I do look forward to working with you to achieve, in spite of all the things that I just said, to achieve a more broadly bipartisan support of something that I think we all agree needs to be undertaken. But I do not think you have yet come to us in a way that is appropriate in making that happen.

But I thank the chairman for having this.

Secretary KERRY. Mr. Chairman, can I—I am surprised by that. I want to get a bigger, a better grade from you, Senator. I quote my own testimony.

The CHAIRMAN. He is a tough grader. So, you know?

Secretary KERRY. We ask you now to work closely with us on a bipartisan basis to develop language that provides a clear signal of support for our ongoing military operations against ISIL. The authorization should give the President the clear mandate and flexibility he needs to successfully prosecute the armed conflict against ISIL and affiliated forces.

We have requested that we work together for an AUMF. We are requesting an AUMF.

Senator CORKER. Mr. Secretary, well, I look forward to working with you a little more closely.

Secretary KERRY. Do I get a better grade?

Senator CORKER. A little more explicitly. I will grade on the curve and give you a little bit better ''attaboy.''

Secretary KERRY. The curve? The curve goes up, not down. [Laughter.]

The CHAIRMAN. I am not even going to go there. Let me just say I want to thank you as well on behalf of all of the members. You know, you have a great deal of respect here, and you have acquit yourself most admirably today, even though I think some of these questions are beyond the role of the Secretary of State. And yet you have done a very admirable job of trying to explain to the committee where we are at, where we want to go, and how, hopefully, we can get there.

I certainly continue to welcome, as I have for months in my efforts to try to develop language that can put the administration in a place that is in synch with the Congress toward our collective goal. And I have no—no concern about our collective goal. Our collective goal is to defeat ISIS, and I am convinced that we will.

But I also think that there is a very compelling reason for Congress to act and to express itself, as Senator Kaine has said, months after we already sent sons and daughters of America into harm's way.

I think this hearing has helped us crystallize some of the core issues that are still in difference between the legislative and executive branch, and I would hope that we could find a way to broach them. However, it is the chair's intention to continue a markup on Thursday. If we can work from here to Thursday to further narrow those, those would be great.

But there is a majority of this committee's desire to express themselves on a vote on an authorization of the use of military force. I am going to honor that view and move forward, and we will see where we end up from there.

I am not so sure that we are going to end this week in the session in the Senate. And if we do not, then I would actually argue that there should be a broader debate in the Senate as well. But in any event, we look forward to working with you, Mr. Secretary.

And with the thanks of the committee, this hearing is adjourned.

[Whereupon, at 5:29 p.m., the hearing was adjourned.]

ADDITIONAL MATERIAL SUBMITTED FOR THE RECORD

ARTICLE SUBMITTED BY SENATOR BARBARA BOXER

[From The Daily Beast, Dec. 9, 2014]

ISIS JIHADIS GET ''SLAVERY FOR DUMMIES''

(By Jamie Dettmer)

They've enslaved thousands of Yazidi women—and now the militants must follow "rules" laid out in an awful new list of dos and don'ts, from treatment of virgins to reasons for beating.

Whom can you enslave? What can you do with female slaves? Can you beat them and have sex with them? The militants of the self-styled Islamic State, never shy to parade their gruesome, atavistic interpretation of the Quran and its place as they see it in the modern world, have now answered those questions.

In a long list of the dos and don'ts governing the enslavement and treatment of women and girls captured by jihadi warriors, ISIS includes details of "permissible" sexual practices with female slaves. The new rules follow widespread reports this summer of the jihadis enslaving women from the Yazidi religious minority seized during the militants' lightning offensive in northern Iraq.

Issued Dec. 3 by ISIS's ''Research and Fatwa Department,'' the rules are laid out in question-and-answer format—a kind of ''Slavery for Dummies.'' It is permissible to beat slaves, trade them, and offer them as gifts, to take virgins immediately and to have sex with a pre-pubescent girl, ''if she is fit for intercourse,'' whatever that means.

According to Nazand Begikhani, an adviser to the Kurdistan regional government and researcher at the University of Bristol Gender and Violence Research Center, ISIS has kidnapped more than 2,500 Yazidi women. Yazidi activists, meanwhile, say they have compiled a list of at least 4,600 missing Yazidi women, seized after they were separated from male relatives, who were shot.

The women were bussed, according to firsthand accounts of women who have managed to flee, to the ISIS-controlled cities of Mosul in Iraq and Raqqa in Syria, and chosen and traded like cattle. Kurdish authorities in northern Iraq say they have freed about 100 Yazidi women. In October, ISIS justified its enslavement of the women-and of any non-believing females captured in battle—in its English-language digital magazine *Dabiq*. Islamic theology, ISIS propagandists argued, gives the jihadis the right, much in the same way that the Bible's Ephesians 6:5 tells "Slaves, obey your earthly masters with fear and trembling."

The difference, of course, is that there is no rampaging Christian terror army enslaving women and waving the Bible around now to justify such abuse, although there have been individual Western cultists widely dismissed as cranks or madmen who have sought biblical justification for abuse of women.

In September, 120 senior Muslim scholars, including Sheikh Shawqi Allam, the grand mufti of Egypt, and Sheikh Muhammad Ahmad Hussein, the mufti of Jerusalem and All Palestine, issued a lengthy letter condemning ISIS as un-Islamic. "It is forbidden in Islam to ignore the reality of contemporary times when deriving legal rulings," they argued. And they condemned the mistreatment of the Yazidi and the denial of women's rights.

Below—courtesy of the Washington, D.C.-based the Middle East Media Research Institute, a nonprofit organization that monitors extremism-are some highlights of the ISIS rules governing the enslavement of women and how slaves should be treated.

Question 1: What is al-sabi?

Al-Sabi is a woman from among ahl al-harb [the people of war] who has been captured by Muslims.

Question 3: Can all unbelieving women be taken captive?

There is no dispute among the scholars that it is permissible to capture unbelieving women [who are characterized by] original unbelief [kufr asli], such as the kitabiyat [women from among the People of the Book, i.e. Jews and Christians] and polytheists. However, [the scholars] are disputed over [the issue of] capturing apostate women. The consensus leans toward forbidding it, though some people of knowledge think it permissible. We [ISIS] lean toward accepting the consensus.

Question 4: Is it permissible to have intercourse with a female captive?

It is permissible to have sexual intercourse with the female captive. Allah the almighty said: "[Successful are the believers] who guard their chastity, except from their wives or (the captives and slaves) that their right hands possess, for then they are free from blame [Quran 23:5-6]''.

Question 5: Is it permissible to have intercourse with a female captive immediately after taking possession [of her]?

If she is a virgin, he [her master] can have intercourse with her immediately after taking possession of her. However, is she isn't, her uterus must be purified [first].

Question 7: Is it permissible to separate a mother from her children through [the act of] buying and selling?

It is not permissible to separate a mother from her prepubescent children through buying, selling, or giving away [a captive or slave]. [But] it is permissible to separate them if the children are grown and mature.

Question 9: If the female captive was impregnated by her owner, can he then sell her?

He can't sell her if she becomes the mother of a child.

Question 13: Is it permissible to have intercourse with a female slave who has not reached puberty?

It is permissible to have intercourse with the female slave who hasn't reached puberty if she is fit for intercourse; however, if she is not fit for intercourse, then it is enough to enjoy her without intercourse.

Question 16: Can two sisters be taken together while taking slaves?

It is permissible to have two sisters, a female slave and her aunt [her father's sister], or a female slave and her aunt [from her mother's side]. But they cannot be together during intercourse, [and] whoever has intercourse with one of them cannot have intercourse with the other, due to the general [consensus] over the prohibition of this.

Question 19: Is it permissible to beat a female slave?

It is permissible to beat the female slave as a [form of] darb ta'deeb [disciplinary beating], [but] it is forbidden to [use] darb al-takseer [literally, breaking beating], [darb] al-tashaffi [beating for the purpose of achieving gratification], or [darb] al-ta'dheeb [torture beating]. Further, it is forbidden to hit the face.